Wild Grapes and Rattlesnakes

The Memoirs of a Premature Anti-Fascist

By
George Cullinen

ISBN: 1-4140-4449-6 (e-book)
ISBN: 1-4140-4448-8 (Paperback)

Library of Congress Control Number: 2003099352

This book is printed on acid free paper.

Printed in the United States of America
Bloomington, IN

1stBooks – rev. 01/14/04

DEDICATION

With pride, deep respect and love,
I recall George's ideas and life as being
synonymous with justice and human rights.
The line of his being continues to flow in the course
of the struggle for freedom and peace -- "The Good Fight.".

Sonia Robbins Cullinen

Contents

Foreword
by Edward Asner

George Cullinen is not nice. He's not fair either. He's turned me green with envy and in my usual "poor me" state, I grumble that it's too late to change and emulate him. For he is a Renaissance man, has lived his life accordingly, put it on paper and delighted me by doing so.

We first met at the 60th anniversary of the Lincoln Brigade in New York, where after performing some function and glad handling well-wishers, George introduced himself and asked if I'd read his book. Being later for my next gig and not wanting to offend a member of the Brigade who are the finest people I have ever met despite the fact our government labeled them "premature anti-Fascists," I gave him a hurried "Yes" and a mailing address and left.

I am so honored to have read this book. *Wild Grapes and Rattlesnakes* is a tale of our past century, one which we'll never see the likes of again. A century in which the forces of evil and good were so clearly defined. Cullinen is a man of that century who so simply and clearly strode, or maybe even sauntered along, accepting the challenges and fighting for the people, *la gente,* as he did so.

There is no ego that jumps off these pages, but the accomplishments, the survival of tragedies, the adventures and through it all, the sense of decency and the desire to do good -- all of which make this a sweet and lasting memory.

Perhaps our world has become too jaded and cynical to create future lives like George Cullinen's. If so, God save us.

And I'm still very jealous.

Introduction

Homage to Spain

On November 10, 1996, I traveled to Spain along with 380 fellow veterans of the International Brigades for what was to be our sixtieth anniversary reunion. All of us were survivors of the Spanish Civil War, the bloody conflict that engulfed the country from 1936 to 1939 and was a prelude to the horrors of World War II. We had been among the 42,000 foreign volunteers from twenty-nine countries who came to Spain to fight Fascism, and our return after sixty years represented both a long-belated victory and a vindication of the democratic ideals that brought us here in the first place.

Like many of my comrades, I came back without any expectations beyond the anticipated pleasure of our seeing each other again, as we had on various occasions through the years. But this time we were embraced by the people of Spain with such a passionate outpouring of good will that we were overwhelmed by the reception afforded us. We were to be granted honorary citizenship by Spain's parliament, and from the moment that we arrived in Madrid, we found ourselves in the middle of a spirited celebration the likes of which I had never seen. With the media spotlight trained on us, we were inundated by music and fanfare. Bands greeted us and exultant crowds showered us with flowers and gifts.

Stepping back onto Spanish soil and into this jubilant atmosphere, I was flooded by memories and had the feeling my life had come full circle. I knew there was one fellow veteran among my American comrades to whom I owed that life. We met again that first morning in the lobby of the Hotel Convencion. Like myself, Nate Thornton had been a merchant seaman and waterfront labor organizer who volunteered to serve with the Abraham Lincoln Brigade, the American contingent of the International Brigades. Both of us had arrived in Spain in 1937 and saw action during the battle of Brunete. At a certain point in that campaign, I had suffered a breakdown on the battlefield, mentally overcome by what was called back then "battle fatigue" or "shell shock." My condition would have made me a dead man that day had it not been for Nate, who hauled me into an ambulance and somehow managed to get me to a hospital.

In our hotel lobby all these years later, I recognized him at once. This was the man to whom I had owed such an enormous debt of gratitude my entire life. There were hugs and backslaps that morning, and I introduced Nate to my wife Sonia, who was by my side as she has been for more than six decades now. Looking at Nate, I could see the passage of years, but the same warmth and spirit still animated his smile, and for a moment his features defied time and age. He called me, "Whitey," the nickname my blonde hair and fair complection had won for me in my youth. Wishing to acknowledge the debt at last and thank him properly, I tried to remind Nate of our battlefield encounter. "You saved my life that day," I told him.

He was surprised by my words and looked uncertain for a moment, brows furrowed. Then he said flatly, "I don't remember what happened, Whitey. There were so many wounded on that battlefield."

"I was in shock," I recalled, "and you transported me to a field hospital."

"I may have," he said, "but I have no memory of it."

In my eyes his memory lapse in no way diminished his act of courage. If anything, his not remembering those men like me who he saved only magnified the selfless humanity of his actions. I told him, "You've always been a hero to me, Nate. All these years you and Spain have been a part of my life." That was true. My political and ethical compass brought home from that terrible battlefield has guided me through the years as I recount them in this book, and the same has been true for many of my comrades. None of us who survived those killing fields ever thought of ourselves as heroes – the gratitude we felt just to have come through alive has always demanded our shared humility.

"I don't feel like I was any hero," Nate demurred with soft-spoken modesty. "There were others who were much braver than I ever was in the war. I was just driving an ambulance every day back and forth to the front."

Nate was twenty-two when he decided to risk his youth for the cause that united us all. He and his father, Mark, both came to Spain in 1937 by crossing the Pyrenees together on foot. As far as I knew, they were the only father and son team in the Brigades. Mark ran a Madrid tire-repair operation to salvage the ancient vehicles that the anti-Fascist forces desperately needed at the time to support the war effort. He left the country four months before Nate departed at the end of 1938.

Like me, Nate would carry his ideals with him the rest of his life as a political activist on the home-front. Neither of us ever had doubts about coming here to put our lives on the line for the ideals of liberty in which we believed. Like most of our comrades-in-arms, we were a simpler breed than that conflicted hero, Robert Jordan, the American volunteer who Hemingway depicted as being tormented by doubts in the novel, *For Whom the Bell Tolls.* Our faith in the cause was passionate but never blind. We came from all walks of life and were as diverse a group as the countries we represented. Heeding the call of Spain's Republican government for help in its hour of need, our small numbers constituted a moral force that ultimately inspired the world.

By returning to Spain, we were in reality accepting a prophetic invitation that had been made when the last of us departed from Spain in November of 1938. At the farewell parade to the Brigades in Barcelona that year, the Spanish patriot and Communist Party leader, Dolores Ibarruri (also known as *La Pasionaria*, or Passion Flower), addressed us as follows: "Comrades of the International Brigades! Political reasons, reasons of State, the welfare of that same cause for which you offered your blood with boundless generosity, are sending you back, some of you to your own countries and other to forced exile. You can go proudly. You're history. You are legend. You are the heroic example of democracy's solidarity and universality. We shall not forget you, and when the olive tree of peace puts forth its leaves again, mingled with the laurels of the Spanish Republic's victory – come back!"

And so we had come back. On the first night celebrating our return, Madrid's sports stadium, El Palacio De Los Desportes, was filled with thousands of cheering Madrileños of all ages. The evening was highlighted by impassioned speeches, Garcia Lorca poems, mournful flamenco and Spanish, French, German, and Italian battle songs. I attended with Sonia, and as the festivities progressed, many of us found ourselves in tears. We *brigadistas* saluted the crowd and once again raised our clenched fists -- *puños en alto* -- to acknowledge a cause that has long been called "the good fight," and rightly so. With thunderous ovations, the Spanish people expressed their gratitude for the part we had played in their struggle to defend the fledgling Spanish Republic against the combined military forces of Franco, Hitler, and Mussolini. Our rallying cry in the war, "*No pasarán!*" – "They shall not pass!" was taken up again that night in a mass demonstration of solidarity.

During the next ten days we attended daily receptions in our honor and visited many of the war memorials, monuments, and cemeteries scattered throughout Madrid, Barcelona and Albacete. Everywhere we were met with cheers, music, outstretched arms and emotional embraces. My wife remembers being lifted into the air by the exuberant crowds. We passed through them with fists raised again and again in triumphant salute, deeply touched by the warmth and enthusiasm of those who honored us.

The decision to grant us citizenship had been approved by a unanimous vote of the parliament thanks to a right-wing contingent who walked out in protest. Apparently, there were still a few unrepentant souls who had been supporters of Franco's totalitarian regime. Despite them, this historic act called for a nationwide fiesta, *Homenaje a las Brigadas Internacionales, 1936-1939* (Homage to the International Brigades, 1936-1939). A committee of friends known as Los Amigos de las Brigadas Internacionales raised approximately a million dollars to cover the expenses for the veterans and their spouses who made the trip. After more than half a century, some of us were barely able to walk. Others were in wheelchairs. Some were missing limbs, and most one way or another still carried inward scars. But all of us had been determined to make this historic trip, and with the generous support of the Amigos, we were here.

Everywhere we Brigade survivors traveled in Spain, we were photographed and interviewed by journalists, television news crews and documentary filmmakers. They asked us questions like: "Why did you joint the Brigades?" "Where did you fight?" "How do you feel now about what you did so many years ago? Would Hitler have been stopped early had you won in Spain?"

In some cases, our answers became sixty second sound-bites that cruelly diminished what the actual experience had been for us. My own answers set forth in these pages require me to retrace the path that brought me to Spain, a journey that began in the early years of the last century. I place this account alongside those that others have written in the hope that our collective memories will allow us to commemorate the unsung heroes like Nate Thornton and the many thousands of others who we left behind in their graves. I write of them lest we forget, and perhaps no more fitting eulogy was ever written than that by Langston Hughes dedicated to the volunteers who died in Spain:

I came
Crossing an Ocean,
And half a continent.
Borders
And mountains, as high as the heavens,
And governments who told me: NO!
YOU CANNOT GO!
I came.
In the luminous frontiers of tomorrow
I put the strength and wisdom
Of my years,

Not much,
Since I am young.
(I should have said, was young,

Because I'm dead).

I've given what I want to,

And what I had to give

So that others would live.

And when the bullets

Stopped my heart

And the blood

Flooded my throat,

I didn't know if it was blood,

Or a red flame?

Or simply my death

Become life?

It's all the same"

Our dream!

My death!

Your life!

Our blood!

A flame!

It's all the same.

Chapter One

Pacific Roots / 1914 - 1931

Why at the age of twenty-two did I volunteer to fight in Spain? What led me to that youthful act of conscience that was to shape the rest of my life? Looking back now and sifting through the jumble of memories, I can see how my personal convictions and destiny were forged in that distant span of years between the First World War and the Great Depression. Yet at the time I was living through the early events of my life, I could not have foreseen how the rough and tumble of fate would carry me to the trenches of Spain. Only with hindsight do my earliest memories provide some hint of the path I would choose and the man I was to become.

The images I carry with me from childhood trace back to California and the Pacific Northwest, where my family was rooted and uprooted many times during my youth. I was born in San Francisco on October 29, 1914 at what is now the University of California Hospital. Back then it was a small teaching hospital overlooking the city from Parnassus Heights. My mother, Eunice Ensign Cullinen, was eighteen years old, and according to my birth certificate, she and my father, George Ambrose Cullinen, lived on Ashbury Street about a block north of Haight Street, at the time a respectable, middle class neighborhood. We stayed there less than a year. My childhood unfolded against the backdrop of World War I, and we were constantly moving up and down the state, most likely because my father's fortunes as a traveling salesman were ever shifting both during and after the war years.

My first real memory goes back to San Diego, where we lived in a small bungalow for a short time. I have only a few brief, tantalizing images of me as a toddler playing in a sandbox in the front yard. I couldn't have been more than three years old. With pail and shovel in hand, I was just outside the front window where my mother could keep her watchful eye on me from inside the house. My playtime that afternoon was interrupted by a noisy crowd of strangers who came marching up the street. They were shouting in Spanish and wore *sombreros* and *serapes.* Their strange language and clothing caught my attention, but before curiosity could lead me into their clamorous path, my mother picked me up and carried me back into the house. The march was no doubt a political demonstration of some kind, my first close encounter with the social unrest and turmoil that was to escalate in the years ahead.

My father came from a world of wealth and privilege. The Cullinen family made a fortune in Canada in the late nineteenth century importing textiles, what were then called "dry goods," which included everything from Irish linens to English woolens. The family business was centered in St. Stephen, New Brunswick, where the Cullinens were long regarded as pillars of the community. They also owned a small boatyard and built some fine old "downeast" schooners. In my way I would carry on that tangent of family tradition when I later shipped out to sea.

My grandfather, Hugh Cullinen, was from County Tyrone in Northern Ireland, where he had married a Scottish lass named Marie MacTavish. They migrated to Canada and settled in St. Johns, New Brunswick. By the time my father was born, Hugh had made enough money to move the family to a grand Victorian mansion in St. Stephen, where my father spent his childhood and adolescence along with two older brothers, Victor and Alexander, and four older sisters, Florence, Alice, Emma, and Mary.

My father was a rich man's son afforded every advantage in life, but he grew up determined to find his own way in the world. He was enough of an adventurer that he left home to take part in the Klondike gold rush, and though he never struck it rich, I remember him in later years showing me a little leather pouch filled with gold nuggets that he kept for sentimental reasons. He had also tried his hand selling dry goods in the Hawaiian Islands, and later, after surviving the 1906 earthquake in San Francisco, he moved to the town of Red Bluff, California and became general manager of Cohn and Kimball's department store.

The store, with its impressive clock tower, was a town landmark that stood on the corner of Main and Walnut streets. That was where he met my mother. Eunice Ensign had recently returned to Red Bluff after graduating from the Aquinas Academy, a Catholic boarding school in Tacoma, Washington. She was fresh from the convent and sweet sixteen, which was a marriageable age in those days. My father was also Catholic, and his position and breeding made him a very desirable match for my mother. A whirlwind courtship led to their engagement and wedding, after which the young couple struck out on their own and moved to San Francisco, where my father was to sell dry goods for the Walton N. Moore Company.

Three years after I was born, my parents returned to the city by the bay and took an apartment on Hayes Street, a block west of Divisadero. I remember trips that I was allowed to take alone on my tricycle to the corner meat market to buy lamb chops, and excursions with my mother by trolley car to the beach and the rugged cliffs overlooking Seal Rock. I'll never forget the excitement that same year when the war ended. People ran into the streets shouting and banging pots and pans. Church bells rang, and whistles blew in the harbor. My parents took me for a ride on a crowded trolley car to see the fleet. I don't remember seeing any ships, only the legs of the grownups surrounding me, and yet even as a boy I was aware that something momentous was taking place.

Back in those days there was a steamship company called the Alexander Line that operated several passenger ships along the coast between San Diego and Seattle. Each vessel was named after a member of the shipowner's family -- the *SS Ruth Alexander,* the *SS Emma Alexander,* and so forth. Just after the war, my mother took me on one of those company ships to visit her mother in Tacoma. American troops were returning from Europe, and shortly after we arrived, there was a victory parade that passed under the window of our room in the Berkshire Hotel. I leaned out and waved a little American flag, thrilled to watch the colorful spectacle of marching troops, artillery and "Whippet" tanks.

That same evening another parade passed under our window. This one was a demonstration by the International Workers of the World (IWW). Much later I learned that the "Wobblies," as they were known, had been agitating for the return of American troops from Siberia. An American Expeditionary Force (AEF) had been sent there to fight the Bolsheviks, and the

IWW organized anti-war protests in Tacoma and other cities. Once again with enthusiasm, I waved my little flag from our window, of course, without yet having the slightest comprehension of the history I was witnessing.

We visited my grandmother again in the fall of 1919 when my mother was in the early stages of her second pregnancy. I remember going on a picnic one day to Wright's Park with my mother and grandmother and a small group of family friends. I was playing with a little girl about my age by the edge of a lake when I suddenly decided to push her into the water. As soon as she fell in, I knew I had done something terribly wrong. Hearing her screams, I hid in some bushes and watched as one of our picnic group, a soldier back from Europe, waded into the lake and pulled her to safety. Later, I heard my name being called and sheepishly wandered back expecting to be punished. But to my surprise, the adults remained unaware that I was the culprit. They were relieved just to know that I was safe, and I wasn't about to tell anyone what I had done. Like many children, I carried my share of deep, dark secrets.

There were other mischievous antics on my part that drove my poor mother to distraction. With my father away at work most days, she was the one who bore the brunt of my childish shenanigans. Yet my father's absence didn't protect me from his stern, old-fashioned ideas about child rearing. Whenever he came home and my mother informed him of my misdeeds, I could expect to feel the sting of his razor strap on my backside. In the fall of 1919, my parents put me in kindergarten, which I remember as a dimly lit, overcrowded room where I shared a desk with another boy. Walking up and down the aisles with ruler in hand was a Catholic nun. I managed to escape the sting of that ruler on my first day by making a getaway over a fence during recess, then stealing a tricycle and pedaling home.

Later when I was found out, I counted myself lucky to be given bread and milk for supper and then sent to bed early, without suffering the dreaded lash of my father's strap.

On March 3, 1920, my mother gave birth to a healthy baby boy, Richard MacTavish Cullinen. My brother never got to know our mother because she died a week later from injuries received while trying to escape from the hospital. Suffering from some form of postpartum psychosis, she had been locked in her room by the hospital staff. Apparently, it never occurred to them that she might try to go out the window. But that's exactly what she did, ending her young life on the front steps of the hospital.

I heard the news when a next door neighbor shouted from her window that something horrible had happened to my mother. I didn't understand her words, but her tone conveyed enough to strike terror in a five year old boy. My grandmother, Maybelle Hatfield Ensign, soon arrived from Tacoma to take care of me and my newborn brother. My mother's first cousin, whom I called Aunt Dude, came from Red Bluff to lend a hand. My father was away at the time, and I would see him only sporadically for the rest of my life. He provided for me and my brother for a number of years, sending checks to my grandmother from wherever he happened to be. In the days and weeks after my mother's funeral, my grandmother became the maternal authority figure for me and my brother. She soon packed us up and moved us to Red Bluff.

We stayed at Aunt Dude's place a few weeks, and there I got to know my great grandmother, Susan Van Landingham Hatfield, who lived in a little house nearby. She was in her late eighties and lived alone except for an old yellow dog named Rock and a cow in the back yard named Bossie. The image of my great grandmother teaching me how to milk that cow with a tin cup could have made for a Norman Rockwell portrait. She had grown up in Pennsylvania Dutch country and was part of the great wave of settlers who made the journey to California in the 1850's by covered wagon. I can still vividly recall her holding me on her lap in a rocking chair and singing in German, comforting me without my understanding a single word.

About a month after my mother died, some Norwegian friends of my grandmother's showed up in an enormous Packard touring car and drove us to Tacoma. We stayed for the next few months in a magnificent old mansion near Point Defiance Park. Still numb with shock over the loss of my mother, I spent hours lying on a couch in the living room, listening over and over to a phonograph record of John McCormack singing "I'll Take You Home Again, Kathleen." At the end of the summer in 1920, we left Tacoma in a Pullman car on the fabled Shasta Limited of the Southern Pacific Railroad. The trip back to Red Bluff took two days, and we had sleeping berths. In the California resort town of Shasta Springs, we got off the train to drink the natural spring water, which many people believed had healing powers. For my grandmother, this was a kind of religious ritual like making a pilgrimage to Lourdes.

After we settled back in Red Bluff that fall, I started first grade at Lincoln Grammar School, but my schooling was soon interrupted. In the next five years, we moved at least seven times between Red Bluff and Tacoma, and with each move I was sent to a different school and had to make new friends. In Red Bluff, we lived in three different houses. In Tacoma, I can recall two houses, two apartments and one hotel room. I have fond memories of riding that city's trolley cars and visiting its harbor bustling with ships, and being taken to vaudeville shows at the Pantages Theater, and devouring delicious ice cream concoctions at a popular spot called the

Pig 'n Whistle. I boarded at Tacoma's Aquinas Academy, the same school where my mother had received her Catholic education. With the sexes strictly segregated, the only female contact I had there was with the nuns. One of them, Sister Angela, had been a mentor to my mother and taught her to play the harp. The gentle sister became something of a guardian angel to me, often inviting me to her quarters in the evening to listen as she played her instrument.

During our last year in Tacoma, I became an altar boy at St. Leo's school. After serving Mass, I was sometimes invited to breakfast in the priest's house next to the church. I might have become a candidate for the priesthood, but that was never to be, even as hooked as I was on Catholicism at that point. St. Leo's was some distance from where we lived, and at the age of eight, I traveled alone to and from school by cable car and trolley, a measure of my boyish independence. I was a good student without yet having any idea what I might want to be in the world. Not long after my ninth birthday, we left Tacoma for the last time and moved back to Red Bluff, our permanent home for the next four years.

My grandmother Maybelle Hatfield Ensign had four sisters, Lillie, Eleanor, Emma, and Jessie; and three brothers, Andrew, Earl, and Fred. The brothers all lived in or near Red Bluff, as did Aunt Emma. Aunt Lillie lived on a houseboat on the Puget Sound. Her floating home was moored alongside a dock in the harbor, not far from the big totem pole which was one of Tacoma's main tourist attractions. She was married to a man named Ed Smith who was an organizer for the IWW. Once while we were living in Red Bluff, Uncle Ed blew into town on a freight train, came to our house, took a bath, put on clean clothes, and took me and my brother to the candy store to buy us ice cream cones. From that day on, I thought the Wobblies must be among the best people in the world.

During our years in Red Bluff, my grandmother had a long romance with a man named Clyde Shaw, who spent more time with us during that period than my father did. Clyde was a house painter and paperhanger who had done the work on our first house in Red Bluff. His relationship with my grandmother was carried on discreetly in accord with what was then considered "proper." I wondered at times why they never married, and perhaps the reason was that my grandmother knew that she was seriously ill and that her days were numbered. Nevertheless, she and Clyde often took us for rides in his Maxwell in the evenings, usually stopping at an ice cream parlor for milkshakes on the way home. An avid sportsman, Clyde took me with him to hunt quail and wild doves. Thanks to those outings, I felt close to the land and learned a healthy respect for the wonders of nature that later in life came back to spur my increasing concerns for the environment.

At the end of the summer of 1924, we moved into a grand two-story house at the corner of Lincoln and Cedar Streets. I don't know where my grandmother found the money to buy the house, but I suspect my father helped from a distance. From that point on, my memories of Red Bluff are filled with uncles, aunts, cousins, dogs, cattle, sheep, rodeos, circus parades with steam calliopes, birthday and Halloween parties, joining the Boy Scouts, climbing trees and running naked in the woods with my friends, riding bareback and reading the funny papers on Sunday mornings, picking wild flowers in the spring, picking figs and pomegranates in the summer and persimmons in the fall. With pencils and crayons, I drew pictures of Mount Lassen to the east of town and snow-covered Mount Shasta, which loomed on the northern horizon like a giant strawberry ice cream cone.

Wild Grapes and Rattlesnakes

Thanks to our extended family, my brother and I had relatively stable and happy childhoods despite our many relocations. Our father managed to visit us for a few days every Christmas, always arriving with a big bag of presents. We were treated to traditional, mouth-watering Christmas dinners, with roast turkey, cranberry sauce and all the trimmings, homemade mince pies and plum pudding with hard sauce. Those were happy times when family and friends gathered to share the hard-won fruits of their labor. Much of what we ate was raised and grown by those same people who sat at my grandmother's dinner table. All of that was an America that no longer exists, yet it was that deep-rooted sensibility and system of values that entered my bloodstream and stayed with me wherever I traveled in life.

During our summers in Red Bluff, Aunt Dude was always busy with her Ball Mason jars, putting up vegetables and preserving fruit for the winter. One of her specialties was a jelly made from the wild grapes that grew abundantly near a swimming hole called Antelope Creek, east of town toward Mount Lassen. We would go there on summer days to cool off and pick grapes. I was always warned to be careful of rattlesnakes that lurked in the shade of the vine-covered Cottonwood trees. Once, while blithely picking away, I was suddenly grabbed by one of the adults and catapulted in the air to a spot about ten feet away. I had been standing unaware of a huge rattler coiled at my feet and ready to strike. The men waded into the underbrush with clubs and pounded the life out of it. Then they held up the dead snake for us to see. It was a real killer, with seven rattles and a button. I was told there was enough venom in those fangs to have put a slow and painful end to me. Even so, whenever I tasted Aunt Dude's grape jelly, I knew those wild grapes were more than worth the risk, a simple childhood lesson that I would one day take with me to Spain.

After skipping seventh grade, I completed grammar school and began my freshman year at Red Bluff Union High School. I managed to keep up with my studies despite having to care for my grandmother, who by the summer of 1927 was bedridden with cancer and completely dependent on my help. Each day I fed her, emptied her bedpan and made sure that she took her medication. Relatives helped as much as they could, but they had their own families and responsibilities at home. I was relieved at the end of the summer when my father arrived in a brand new Essex and took charge of the situation. He had recently acquired a Hudson-Essex dealership near San Francisco and had the means to hire a full-time practical nurse, who also did the cooking and cleaning for the household.

As a twelve-year-old, I couldn't accept the fact that my grandmother was dying. I tried to make believe that life was returning to normal that summer and rode my bike to the high school every day to swim in the pool. Saturday matinees allowed me to escape into the worlds of Tom Mix, Buck Jones, Felix the Cat, Charlie Chaplin, Harold Lloyd, and Our Gang. In the library, I found other ways to avoid the unpleasant realities at home, devouring books like *When a Man's a Man, Tarzan of the Apes*, *Two Years Before the Mast*, *The Call of the Wild*, and the Tom Swift stories.

At the end of the summer, my grandmother's condition worsened. She was only forty-eight when a priest came to her bedside to administer Extreme Unction. In fact, she had converted to Catholicism at the last minute and requested that the sacraments be given to her. I can still remember how the withering sound of her death rattle could be heard everywhere in the house during her last hours. This second traumatic loss came like an unexpected blow from behind and changed our lives forever. After the funeral, my father quickly stepped in to make arrangements for me and my brother.

We could have stayed in Red Bluff with relatives, but that idea didn't meet with our father's approval. With his Scottish-Irish Catholic background, he wanted to protect us from the influence of the wild and woolly sheepherders, cowboys, atheists, agnostics, Seventh Day Adventists, and Wobblies on my mother's side of the family. He piled us and our belongings into his Essex and headed south, first dropping my seven-year-old brother off at a Catholic boarding school in the town of Benicia. I then spent the next two weeks with my father in a cheap hotel in San Francisco waiting for an answer to a newspaper ad that he placed. That was how he found the Farrells, a good Irish Catholic family who agreed to take me in.

I spent the next three and a half years with the Farrells. During that time I attended St. Ignatius High School and was indoctrinated by the Jesuits, serving as an altar boy at St. Ignatius Cathedral. The solemn high masses and regular confessions and communions were in my case a kind of perverse therapy for guilt brought on by the uncontrollable sex drive of a healthy adolescent. I was more and more preoccupied with fear of going to Hell and the need to be free of mortal sin. It wasn't until my first encounter with the opposite sex a few years later that I would decide in favor of going to Hell.

The Farrells lived in a three-story, wood-frame Victorian house on the corner of Hayes and Lyon Streets. I shared a room with their youngest son Bill, a senior at St. Ignatius. Bill had an older sister who was still living at home, and two older brothers who had moved away. There were also two older men, Mr. Sherry and Mr. Gray, who rented rooms on the second floor. Mr. Sherry, an Austrian, was the chef at the Southern Pacific General Hospital across the street. Mr. Gray, an orderly at the hospital, was a quiet

Irishman. The two boarders were the Farrells' main source of income.

They were lower-middle-class, second and third generation Irish immigrants, all of them hardworking. Even Bill sold newspapers after school, a job I inherited after he finished high school and found work downtown. Mr. Farrell was legally blind, retired, and living on a pension. He stayed home most of the time and helped run the household, but Mrs. Farrell carried most of the burden. A strong, heavyset woman, she was ever cheerful and had a way of making everyone feel at home. I was soon a full-fledged member of the family. I remember doing on my homework at the dining room table after dinner, and when I had time, lying on the couch listening to a crystal radio set with earphones.

As a freshman at St. Ignatius, I fell behind the rest of my class, unable to keep up with the rigorous demands of my Jesuit teachers after the recent upheaval in my life. I flunked that year and had to repeat it the next. In 1928, a freshman again, I won medals in Latin and algebra and was at the head of my class. I joined the school band, made the track team and showed every outward sign of having adjusted to my new life and family.

Outside of school and the church, I was drawn to a gang of older boys who Bill hung out with. They usually congregated on a corner in front of a candy and cigar store owned by a German-American family, the Odenthals. Two of the Odenthal boys were members of the gang. They called themselves the Beachcombers Club and often met in the Farrells' basement to play poker. I was dying to be accepted into the club, and eventually I was allowed to tag along. I most enjoyed spending summer days with the gang at Deadman's Cove near Mile Rock Lighthouse. The cove served as a very isolated nude beach and private domain for the Beachcombers Club. To get there we had to climb like mountain goats down a very narrow trail on a steep hill overlooking the ocean.

The sea had already taken hold of me. I can still feel myself holding my breath while diving headlong into an eight-foot wave. I can smell the fresh seaweed and kelp on the beach and feel the soft wet sand while walking barefoot through the incoming tide. I can hear the barking of seals and sea lions, the shrill cry of gulls, the deep *basso profundo* of the lighthouse foghorn. I can see ships heading out to sea, beckoning to me, and the fog rolling in at the end of the day.

I remember fishing off the end of a dock in San Francisco Bay and bringing home my catch, usually porgies or perch, to Mrs. Farrell who would cook them for our dinner. The Bay area offered no end of delights for a young man. There was playing tennis in Golden Gate Park and riding horseback in Visitacion Valley, playing touch tackle with the Beachcombers at the Marina, riding the cog railway to the top of Mt. Tamalpais and then hopping, skipping and leaping all the way down the mountainside to end up in the quiet splendor of Muir Woods.

Those idyllic days came to an abrupt halt for me in the winter of 1930, a year after the stock market crashed. When the Depression claimed my father's automobile business, he could no longer pay my tuition at St. Ignatius, nor could he long afford the price of my board and room with the Farrells. My world was soon turned upside down once again.

After dropping out of high school at age sixteen and working a few part-time jobs in the city, I landed a steady job as an errand boy in Samuel's Jewelry Store on Market Street. There I became friendly with Mrs. Peterson, the cashier. She was married to a sea captain, and I confided to her about my adolescent seagoing fantasies. Mrs. Peterson took a maternal interest in me, and it wasn't long before I found myself invited to her home for dinner and to meet Captain Peterson when he was in port. Her idea was for her husband to interview me and determine if I might be a good candidate for officer training in the Merchant Marine. Steamship companies at that time took aboard cadets who after serving three years at sea could become third mates. The opportunity of a secure future as a licensed officer with one of the leading steamship companies could not to be passed up.

My interview won the captain's approval and in March of 1931, I signed on as deck cadet on the *SS Surinam,* a United Fruit Company passenger ship under the command of Captain Lars P. Hansen. I was overjoyed with my good fortune, but no one was more pleased than my father, who may have been reminded of his own youthful adventures in the Klondike. He managed to completely outfit me for the job -- sea boots and oilskins, dungarees, underwear, socks, a pea coat, a watch cap, a sweater, and three uniforms -- one navy and two white for the tropics. On the morning of my departure, my father proudly escorted me aboard the ship, introduced me to Captain Hansen, and then said goodbye.

I was shown to a stateroom amidships that I was to share with another cadet who was a couple of years older and already an experienced seaman. On the afternoon of that first day, I was assigned to stand gangway watch, a duty that I took less than seriously. For the benefit of arriving passengers, bunches of ripe bananas had been placed on the promenade deck near the gangway, and by the end of the afternoon, I managed to gorge myself on the forbidden fruit. I avoided any sort of reprimand, but my frivolous attitude didn't bode well for me.

Once we put to sea, my first assignment was to learn seamanship by working on deck during the day with the bo's'n and the sailors, most of whom were Scandinavian. At the end of a day of chipping rust, red-leading, painting, caulking decks, splicing rope, washing down, holystoning, and polishing brass, I cleaned up and changed from dungarees to a fresh, white uniform. I then sat down for dinner at the officers' table in the passengers' dining salon. After dinner, I went up to the bridge to learn how to steer the ship, box the compass, take an azimuth of the setting sun, and so on.

From the beginning it was made clear to me by my superiors -- Mr. Paulsen, Mr. "Rope Yarn" Johnson, and Mr. Welch -- first, second, and third mates respectively, that I was not allowed to fraternize with the unlicensed personnel either aboard ship or when we went ashore in foreign ports. This was all a routine part of my training to become a third mate. But as a sixteen-year-old dropout from a Jesuit high school with an absentee father, I needed role models and allies, and I would eventually have to choose between the officers and common seaman.

I was most influenced by the older men I worked with on deck every day -- the bo's'n and the sailors -- and I soon became aware of the contrast between their living conditions and those afforded the officers. The sailors slept in a crowded fo'c'sle with double-decker bunks, while each officer had his own stateroom. The sailors took their baths with a bucket of water heated with live steam. As an officer in training, I had a first class stateroom amidships with a tub and a shower. The sailors' meals were served in a tiny mess room back aft; their food was canned, and often cockroaches would appear in their bread or muffins. I ate like a gourmet in the passengers' dining salon. Sailors' wages were a disgrace -- $30 a month for an OS (ordinary seaman) and $45 a month for an AB (able-bodied seaman). In those days, there was no such thing as overtime pay.

Despite the miserable conditions, these hardy seafaring men were able to laugh and roll with the punches as they joked about "The Great White Fleet: plenty of work and nothing to eat." Sometimes their simmering resentment found an outlet while a sailor stood lookout on the bow on a dark night. Every half hour, the helmsman would strike the bells from the wheelhouse, and the lookout would answer on the bell from the fo'c'sle head. After checking the port and starboard running lights and the masthead lights, the lookout would yell to the mate on the bridge, "The lights are bright, sir!" and the mate would answer, "A-a-a-ll right!" But sometimes on a stormy night, the lookout would yell, "Fuck your wife, sir!" and the mate, unable to distinguish the words above the sound of the wind and sea, would answer, "A-a-a-ll right!" When they let me in on this little secret, I knew I had won their trust.

And so it was that these rough-and-tumble Norwegian sailors taught me the rudiments of marlinspike seamanship and became my heroes. These were my shipmates, honest and hardworking to a man. Why should I ignore them when we happened to meet ashore? I quickly learned what sailors do when they go ashore, drinking beer and rum and trying to get laid in every port. My high spirits and lack of maturity caused me to disgrace my uniform more than once by returning aboard drunk. For that folly and breach of discipline, I paid a price.

The day of reckoning came when as a sixteen-year-old cadet I found myself unable to perform my duties on the bridge while traversing the Panama Canal. We had already made four round trips in five months. Then, after seventy-two hours of carousing during shore leave with no sleep, I was assigned to stand by the ship's telegraph, which relayed the pilot's orders from the bridge to the engine room. That night soon after I took the watch, my head nodded and my knees buckled, and the angry pilot had to yell at me to get my attention. Much to my shame, Captain Hansen ordered me to go below and get some sleep.

As soon as we returned to San Francisco, I was told to pack my gear and leave the ship. I had been fired. Now I was homeless, almost broke and heading toward skid row like much of the rest of the country. Whatever else I may have been, I was no prodigal son. I was far too head-strong to turn to my father or family for help. Whatever I was going to learn in life, I was resigned to learn the hard way, and I had not yet given up my seafaring dreams.

Chapter Two

Radicalization at Sea / 1931 - 1936

On my first night back in San Francisco, I quickly made several new friends -- Jimmy Stuart, Frank Hartwell, and Bud Fisher -- who helped me spend my payoff of about $25 in a seedy skid row bar. I treated everyone to rounds of drinks and the next morning woke up in Jimmy's garage. I then moved into Bud's house and was treated like family until I found another job. In October of 1931, I shipped out again, this time as an ordinary seaman on the *SS San Mateo* of the United Fruit Company.

Now that I was a common sailor, I utilized what I had learned as a cadet and wholeheartedly threw in my lot with my unlicensed shipmates. One day the bo's'n, an old-timer from Maine, asked me if I could drive a winch. I said, "Sure I can," anxious to show off my skill. We were cleaning the aft holds and dumping everything overboard. My job was to raise a slingload of dunnage up from the hold and then lower it down as the boom was being swung out over the rail. Another sailor stood by to release the load into the sea as the bo's'n ran back and forth supervising the operation. Everything went fine until the ship took a sudden roll to starboard just as I lowered away, causing the slingload to swing out and plunge into the sea. We were moving at twelve knots with that heavy load dragging like an anchor, imperiling the ship. Pandemonium set in and I stood helplessly listening to the bo's'n rant and rave at me, "Oh sure, you can drive a winch, all right!" It was miraculous that we didn't lose the mainmast and that no one was hurt, but that was the end of my winch-driving career on the *San Mateo.*

The trip lasted only a month, and I once again found myself in San Francisco struggling to survive "on the beach," waterfront slang for being in port and waiting to ship out again. After living hand-to-mouth for three months, I finally signed on the *SS La Perla* bound for Corinto, Nicaragua. The ship happened to be under the command of the same Captain Petersen who had recommended me for the cadet's position. Once out to sea, there was no escape for me from the wrath of this little Napoleon who never let me forget that I had betrayed his trust. There was no messboy on United Fruit Company ships in those days. The mess was assigned to an ordinary seaman like me, and on that trip, the skipper made sure that I took on those extra duties. In addition to standing my regular sea watches, I was responsible for setting the tables, carrying the meals from the galley amidships across the deck to the messroom aft, bussing the dirty dishes back to the galley, and cleaning the "head."

The fact that I managed to pull my weight only aggravated my tormentor all the more. One evening around sunset while we were homeward bound, the skipper called me up to the bridge. With the chief mate and helmsman looking on, Captain Peterson exploded, "Do you know what you are, Cullinen? You're a dirty goddamned son-of-a-bitch!" I stammered, inwardly seething yet helpless to defend myself against his abuse. From that moment on, my attitude toward officers like Peterson was "Fuck your wife, sir." I quit his command as soon as we reached port.

Back on the beach in San Francisco, competition for jobs was cut-throat, and as a seventeen-year-old, I had only seven months of experience at sea. There were men with mate's and skipper's licenses who were willing to take any opening even if it meant sailing in the fo'c'sle. Hiring was conducted off the dock, with one exception. There was a place near the Embarcadero called Fink Hall, a central hiring agency sponsored by the shipowners. The hall was a filthy waiting room that reeked from the stench of winos and "smoke hounds," those human derelicts who drank sterno or "canned heat" as it was called. Legitimate seamen who went to Fink Hall for jobs might spend weeks or months before being hired, provided they were not on the company's blacklist. On days when a ship was due in port, there was usually a crowd of at least a hundred sailors waiting for jobs outside the company shipping master's door at the head of the dock.

I remember standing in that cold hall shivering one morning when the door opened and the shipping master, Terry Lecroix, appeared. He pointed his finger at familiar faces in the crowd around me, shouting gruffly, "You! You! You!" and directed those fortunate sailors into the office. By some miracle, perhaps because there were no more company men available, he picked me. When he had enough men, he said, "Thanks, fellas. See ya," turning his back and closing the door in the faces of those who remained. That morning I signed on the *SS President McKinley* of the Dollar Line as an ordinary seaman for $30 a month.

We were bound for the Hawaiian Islands, Japan, China, and the

Philippines. I was thrilled to be back at sea despite the hardships and cramped quarters. The fo'c'sle was two decks below the main deck and divided between ordinary and able-bodied seaman. I slept on the port side in a room with six double-decker bunks. Twenty-two unlicensed crew were crowded together in a tiny, dungeon-like space. The only ventilation was from a porthole that we had to keep closed most of the time. The able-bodied seaman were aft in a larger room. On the starboard side were rooms for the bo's'n, bo's'n's mate, carpenter, and deck storekeeper. In between were the heads, washrooms, and mess room.

The living and working conditions were hellish, but there was little grumbling and no sign of any trade union organizing. The company had a goon squad onboard that included the bo's'n, the bo's'n's mate, and one able-bodied seaman who was an ex-prize fighter. They intimidated the unlicensed crew by singling out any would-be union organizers and physically working them over, often in front of passengers and officers. These beatings usually took place around sailing time when we were battening down the hatches and securing the booms. The only way to avoid a beating was for a sailor to keep his mouth shut and follow orders, but even that was no guarantee of safety under this arbitrary reign of terror. I tried to subdue my fears as I went ashore in one port after another, taking refuge in the bars and brothels with the rest of my mates. But I couldn't help wondering when my turn would come at the hands of these company thugs.

While on shore leave in Hong Kong, I went along with my watch partner, Jimmy Clark, to pay a visit to a red light district known as Ship Street. Sitting in a bar that night, Jimmy confided to me that he too felt like a marked man. He was planning to jump ship when we reached Kobe, Japan and he invited me to join him. I didn't need to be convinced. Ten years older than I, Jimmy took me under wing and planned our escape down to the last detail, from eluding the customs officers on the dock to finding safe haven ashore.

After the ship tied up at the dock in Kobe, we stole away with our belongings and checked into a small hotel near the waterfront. Then we went to the Corner House Bar in the district of Yoshiwara, known for its barrooms and g*eisha* houses that catered to both foreign and Japanese working men. Jimmy and I were sitting in a booth drinking Asahi beer and celebrating our escape with three geishas dressed in their traditional silk *kimonos.* Jimmy went outside with one of the girls, and I happened to notice that some of the gang from the ship had come into the bar. When I got up to dance with one of my female companions, someone shoved me from behind. As I turned around to see who it was, I felt a stinging blow on the left side of my face. My attacker was, one of the goons, Johnny Lavoie. He was with the bo's'n's mate, Willie Blackwell. Backed up against the bar, I was stunned and at a loss what to do when I saw Jimmy come back inside. Without saying a word, he hurried over and landed a swift, hard right on Johnny's jaw, sending him reeling across the room.

One punch was all it took to solve the problem. A few minutes later, Jimmy and I were in a *goju sen* taxi that took us back to the hotel. At the advice of a kindly *mama san,* I spent the next hour with an ice pack on my face. After a night's sleep, we woke up to the distant sound of the ship's whistle. One long blast told us that she was backing away from the dock into the harbor. We were free, and looking at my grinning face in the mirror that morning, I saw that the ice pack had done its job. Lucky me. No shiner.

Jimmy and I soon moved into a traditional Japanese house in Kamitsusui, a part of Kobe where many foreigners lived. On our behalf, Jim enlisted the aid of his friend, Achi Cameron, who was fluent in Japanese and knew the culture inside out. One evening we had dinner at Achi's home and met his mother, his older sister and their friends. The Camerons lived high on a hill in Kamitsusui in a large two-story, Victorian house overlooking the city and harbor. They were a gracious, hospitable family. We also met Achi's girlfriend Lili, a beautiful young Japanese woman who was carrying on a double romance with Achi and the bo's'n on the *SS President Lincoln.* She was "kept" by the bo's'n, whom she only saw when he was in port, the rest of the time carrying on her clandestine affair with Achi.

The son of a retired American sea captain, Achi had been born and raised in Japan. He was about my age, and I discovered that he too entertained fantasies of going to sea. We became fast friends, and he took great pleasure in introducing Jimmy and me to his country. Sharing a large room on the second floor of our new home, we were soon "going native" -- leaving our shoes at the door, using the *shoji* (sliding paper screens), walking on *tatami* (woven straw flooring), sleeping on futons, sitting on the floor to eat our meals around a small table, and donning *kimonos* and sandals to go for short walks or out to a local restaurant. We wore our Western clothes mostly in the evenings at the dance halls and barrooms, where being American expatriates had a certain cachet even with our limited funds.

I remember going to one of the dance halls with Jim, a smooth dancer, and his Eurasian girlfriend, Marjorie Nishigori, the daughter of a wealthy Japanese government official. The orchestra played mostly Western jazz that night. Although American popular music was beginning to attract Japan's younger generation, the traditional culture was still dominant and I immersed myself in it. The sounds of the *koto* and *samisen* could be heard accompanying the singing voices of *geishas* everywhere early in the evening and late into the night. Local watchmen added a rhythmic note to the atmosphere by clapping two sticks together as they made their rounds of the neighborhood. Those exotic sounds beckoned me and under the spell of their enchantment, I met a geisha named Sachiko, who worked in one of the local bars. Wearing a kimono and sash (*obi)* and wooden clogs *(getah)*, she looked like an exquisite Japanese doll. I was immediately taken with her. Sachiko knew enough English and I had learned enough Japanese by now that we were able to communicate easily and soon fell into an amorous affair.

I remember one of the highlights of the romance was an afternoon hiking trip we made up one of the mountains outside Kobe. Our destination was the Mayasan Hotel, which stood at the summit. There, we had a Western-style lunch and afterwards saw a Japanese movie in the hotel theater. The film told the story of a brave *samurai* warrior defending his lady love against wave after wave of barbaric attackers. I was amused to see the "good guys" won just as they did in our American cowboy movies, with each nation cultivating its own chauvinistic, self-serving mythology without regard for truth. After spending the day on the mountain, we returned in time for Sachiko to work at the bar that night until she was able to join me later on my futon.

This carefree life of bliss came to an abrupt end one morning when Jim and I were stopped in the street by two plainclothes policemen while we were on our way to breakfast. After we identified ourselves, they politely escorted us into a *goju sen* taxi and instructed the driver to take us back to our house for our belongings. The policemen stayed with us until we were incarcerated in a dismal jail cell somewhere on the Kobe waterfront.

Charged with illegal entry into the country, we were to be deported.

We spent the night in an abominable cell. There was a bucket already full of excrement in a dark corner. To be locked up with such filth was doubly shocking to me given the emphasis on cleanliness and decorum otherwise exhibited in Japanese culture. We were fed tea and rice, and shared our cell with an unsavory Japanese character who kept talking about the "coming revolution," a concept that was alien to me at that point. Jimmy and I kept to ourselves, figuring the man was probably a stool pigeon placed with us by the police to find out if we were spies or dangerous subversives.

The next morning we were driven to the office of the American Consul. We had no choice but to sign on the *SS President Grant* and return to San Francisco as "workaways," literally for a penny a month. God knows we earned that penny. In addition to me and Jimmy, there were two other American seamen working for their passage home, one of whom introduced us to marijuana, in my case without any success though I did inhale the forbidden weed. Until we left Kobe, the four of us were confined to a small room amidships that served as a makeshift brig.

The trip took about two weeks, with a twenty-four-hour stopover in Honolulu. Our days were a monotony of chipping rust, redleading, scraping and painting, soogeeing (washing paintwork), holystoning, and washing down decks. We went out in all kinds of weather, with the bo's'n watching us like a hawk. He had no complaints about me because I knew what I was doing. I was proud of my work. None of us got much sleep during the journey because of the noise from the steering engine and the rolling and pitching of the ship.

Our only break was shore leave in Honolulu. We played football on the beach at Waikiki and somehow managed to buy a few bootleg drinks. As always, we were looking for *wahines* (girls), but without luck. Anticipating our homecoming on the mainland, the four of us talked about the problems we had in common like finding a ship and being broke and struggling to make ends meet on the beach. By the time we docked in San Francisco, each of us had a plan, and it was soon every man for himself.

Jimmy decided to return to his family's home in Massachusetts. We said our goodbyes, and his parting words to me were, "Good luck, Whitey. If you ever get back East, don't forget to look me up." I stayed in San Francisco to look for another ship to take me back to Japan, but I soon came down with tonsillitis and wound up in a Marine Hospital run by U.S. Public Health Service. After undergoing a tonsillectomy and short convalescence, I was discharged. On a sunny morning in July, I made my way out the front door and down the steps of the hospital, wondering again where my next meal was going to come from.

I managed to survive with the help of a young German friend, Karl, who had a steady job in the kitchen of the Mark Hopkins Hotel and lived in a small, top-floor walk-up opposite Buena Vista Park. I could have shared my friend's bed easily enough, but I preferred sleeping on the floor in a little alcove, an arrangement that reminded me of the life I had left behind in Japan. Karl and I didn't see each other much because he worked most days while I was out looking for a ship. When we did meet in the evenings, there was always plenty to eat from the hotel kitchen.

After I made a three-week junket to Central America on the *SS Chiriqui,* one of my pals suggested that my knowledge of seamanship might qualify me for a job as a rigger or grip on a Hollywood film crew. That was all I needed to hear. The next day I was on Highway 101 hitchhiking south to Los Angeles. I arrived penniless and hungry. I had never panhandled before, but I was now desperate. On Sunset Boulevard I approached a well-dressed gentleman and asked if he could spare some change for a sandwich and a cup of coffee. He looked me over, reached into his pocket, and pulled out something shiny. I was ready to thank him when I saw that he was holding a police badge. He could have arrested me for vagrancy but instead advised me in no uncertain terms to get out of town. That was the end of my Hollywood fantasy. Two days later I was back at Karl's pad, once again looking for a ship.

I clung to the idea of returning to Japan on the Dollar Line. As luck would have it, the next ship to arrive was the one I had jumped in Kobe, the *SS President McKinley.* I managed to go aboard soon after she was tied up. I had been told that the chances of getting a job were better if you could speak to the bo's'n before he notified the company shipping master. I was ready to swallow my pride and beg for another chance. Much to my surprise, the fearsome slave driver whom I had fled from just a few months before now greeted me like an old friend. He laughed about my jumping ship, but when I asked him for a job he told me, "I'm sorry, Whitey. My hands are tied here in San Francisco. If we were in New York, I could do something for you."

The ship was due to sail in two days to Panama, traveling through the canal and up the East Coast to New York, arriving the third week of October, 1932. I decided to race the *McKinley* across the country. I wanted to be waiting when the ship docked, so I had about three weeks to make the trip. Hitchhiking was easy in California, but after I crossed the Sierras into the desert, there were fewer and fewer rides. I found myself stranded in Winnemucca, Nevada. The only sign of life was a diner where I bummed coffee and donuts. The main street was the highway running through the center of town, and there was no traffic that morning.

I gave up on getting a ride and instead followed the railroad tracks. I found a few guys huddled around a campfire waiting to hop a freight train. I joined them and followed their advice when a train came through, running alongside, then grabbing the rung of a ladder and climbing aboard. Four of us spent the first night in an empty a refrigerator car known as a "reefer." We stayed out of sight to avoid being spotted by company police, those vicious railroad bulls whose reputation for sadism was well-deserved.

By morning, we were in Utah. I rode in an empty boxcar all the way to Salt Lake City, where I found food and shelter thanks to a religious charity group. Listening to a preacher and singing hymns seemed a small price to pay for a hot meal, an army cot and blanket. I traveled on through Colorado by clinging to the outside of an oil tankcar, enthralled by spectacular Rocky Mountain scenery until we entered the six-mile-long Moffatt Tunnel. The narrow space in the tunnel was suddenly filled with clouds of black, suffocating smoke from the coal-burning locomotive. I hung on and covered my face with a bandanna, trying not to breathe too deeply. After what seemed like an eternity, the train pulled out into sunshine and crisp mountain air. When I arrived finally in Denver, I was covered from head to foot with cinders and soot. Now I looked like a real bum.

At the end of my rope again, I turned to panhandling and this time made a success of it, collecting a pile of nickels and dimes as people took pity on what must have looked like a character out of Charles Dickens. One good Samaritan gave me three silver dollars and recommended a cheap hotel where I could get a room and take a bath. I met a couple of World War I veterans who were organizing for the Bonus March protest in Washington, D.C. They told me some stories that shook me up. They said they had fought in the war to make the world safe for democracy, and now like me they were part of the vast army of unemployed that included nearly a third of the work force. Thousands of farmers and their families were being driven off the land by bank foreclosures, thousands of factories and mills were idle, and people everywhere were losing their life savings as bank after bank went belly-up. I wasn't yet ready to embrace the political cause with these radical activists, but much of what they said made sense to me.

I wished them well and continued my race to beat the *SS President McKinley*, riding the rails through Nebraska, Iowa, Illinois, Indiana, and Ohio, finally arriving in Port Jervis, New York. I left the Erie Railroad yard, walked into town and found a bakery on the main street. My disheveled appearance embarrassed me, but I was hungry and went inside. I asked a girl behind the counter if she could give me some stale bread or pastry. Sensing my plight, a gracious woman seated at one of the tables asked me to join her. She introduced herself as Mrs. Schauer, and after listening to my story, she took me across the street to a department store that she owned. She outfitted me with new clothes and arranged for me to stay that night at the YMCA.

Thanks to Mrs. Schauer and her act of generosity, the next morning I was on my way to New York City, riding with the driver in the cab of one of several trailer trucks that she owned. After coming out of the Holland Tunnel into the streets of Manhattan, I was dropped off. I walked along the waterfront down to the Battery only to discover that I was on the wrong side of the Hudson. The Dollar Line piers were across the river in New Jersey.

It was afternoon by the time I finally reached the docks, but there she was, my old ship. She had tied up that morning. Perfect timing, I thought, as I walked past the customs officers. On the docks, longshoremen had already discharged the mail and passengers' baggage and they were now working on the cargo. As I approached the gangway, I saw sailors further down the dock touching up rust spots on the side of the ship. The bo's'n was leaning over the rail on the promenade deck and shouting directions to the sailors below. When he saw me, he did a double take and squinted his eyes in disbelief. He shouted, "What the hell are you doing here? I thought you were in San Francisco."

"Yeah, that's right," I told him, pleased with myself. "But I wanted to get back on the *McKinley,* so I decided to meet you here like you said."

Other sailors were listening and the bo's'n was now on the spot. He told me to wait where I was. As he came toward me, he said, "I'm sorry, Whitey, but we have a full crew. Nobody's quitting." He must have felt that someone who had traveled three thousand miles for a job was at least entitled to an explanation. My hopes were dashed and I was ready to turn around and head back to California. Before embarking on another cross-country trip, I visited an aunt in Montreal and then tried unsuccessfully to look up my old friend Jimmy Clark at his family's home in Massachusetts. I spent a night at the Seamen's House in Boston with dozens of other seafaring men who had been on the beach for months. Talking with them further discouraged me about finding a ship on the East Coast. Before heading west, I decided to stop in Port Jervis to visit the kind woman who had fed and clothed me in my hour of need. Mrs. Schauer welcomed me back and invited me to stay temporarily in an empty apartment she owned. One of her friends owned the local bowling alley, and I worked there briefly as a pin boy.

Early one morning in December, without saying goodbye, I slipped away in a side-door Pullman boxcar on the Erie Railroad. I didn't relish the idea of riding the rails and hitchhiking all the way back to California, but I had no choice. The weather was colder on this trip, and I wasn't dressed for it. The temperature in Kansas City, Missouri hit fifteen degrees below zero. I managed to outfit myself in a shelter run by The Helping Hand Society. Anyone willing to listen to a sermon and sing a few hymns was given a bowl of soup, stale bread and doughnuts and a cot. I soon caught a ride on an oil tankcar heading to Oklahoma and Texas.

On this leg of the journey, I teamed up with a former shipmate of mine, Johnny, who I had run into by chance in Jefferson City. I remember us hanging on through a blinding rainstorm as we rolled into Muskogee, Oklahoma. On Christmas Eve in Dennison, Texas, I panhandled on the main drag. A tall gentleman wearing cowboy boots and a Stetson hat dug down in his pocket and gave me a silver dollar. The following day, Johnny and I walked five miles to the town of Sherman for a free Christmas dinner. After eating our fill, we hopped a freight bound for Fort Worth. As we rumbled south, Johnny took a nap, while I sat with my legs dangling from the boxcar doorway, playing "Red River Valley" on my harmonica, one of the happier moments I remember on that journey.

In Dallas, we spent the night in a hobo jungle near the railroad tracks. The next day there were nearly a hundred people—men, women, and children—waiting by the tracks to catch a freight going west. Suddenly, a half-dozen police vans appeared, and we were surrounded by cops. They herded us into vans and sped away to the city jail. We were thrown into a holding cell known as the "bullpen." The next morning we went to trial, and the judge simply ordered all of us to get out of town. The way it looked to me, attempting to get out of town was a crime in Dallas, and the judge was now ordering us to commit it -- again! And we did, returning to the same place on the tracks, but this time without a cop in sight.

Several days and one freight train later, we were in Douglas, Arizona, boiling up our dirty clothes in another hobo jungle. We wanted to appear respectable for the California immigration patrol. We knew people were being turned away at the state line by the hundreds if they couldn't show proper identification. Fortunately, we both had our ship's discharge papers that proved we had been paid off in the port of San Francisco.

When we reached the state line at Yuma, Arizona, we tried to get a meal before crossing into California. But walking the streets and knocking on doors, we were unable to find a single soul. The town was deserted and we soon gave up our quest for food, catching a freight train that afternoon from Yuma to Indio, then on to Los Angeles, where Johnny and I parted ways. He decided to go on to San Pedro, and I headed north. It would take me three days to hitchhike four hundred fifty miles to San Francisco. Near San Mateo, I found a Salvation Army soup kitchen where I was told, "If you're willing to work, you can have something to eat." I thought that was a fair exchange, and they put me to work on the woodpile. After about an hour, the folks in charge called me and a few other willing workers inside for a meal that was nothing more than stale doughnuts and coffee. When I recall that experience, I hear Pete Seeger singing, "Chop some wood. It'll do you good. You'll get pie in the sky when you die. That's a lie."

I was hungry, tired, and broke when I arrived in San Francisco, but it was nevertheless a relief to be the native son returning to my roots. This was my home port where I had friends and knew my way around.

I resumed my search for a ship going to Japan, but the competition for jobs was worse than ever. After a month of "shaping up" in front of Terry Lacroix's office at Dollar Line pier, I decided to go in and talk to him. I told him that I was willing to take any job in any department. Terry said if I were willing to take a wiper's job in the engine room, he had an opening on the next ship. A wiper's job wasn't what I wanted, but when he told me that the ship was bound for the Far East, that was all I needed to hear. I signed on the *SS President Hoover* as a wiper for $30 a month.

We sailed that same afternoon in February for Honolulu, Yokohama, Kobe, Shanghai, Hong Kong, and Manila. The *President Hoover* and the *President Coolidge* were the newest additions to the Dollar Line's trans-Pacific fleet. They were super ocean liners that carried hundreds of passengers and thousands of tons of cargo. I was savvy enough by now to realize shipping was a business that produced enormous profits for the executives and stockholders of the company, and those profits were all the more enormous thanks to the merchant seamen who kept their ships running while working under slave-like conditions. I was still an undergraduate in the school of hard knocks, but I was learning fast.

As a wiper, I was not only at the bottom of the totem pole in the black gang, those seaman who worked in the engine department, I also spent most of my time at the very bottom of the ship. I was assigned to work in the bilges underneath the engine room floorplates. My job was cleaning up the oil and accumulated filth in preparation for red-leading and painting. The engine room was a living hell. But I did my job and earned the respect of the engine room storekeeper. Even so, I knew I wasn't cut out to be an engineer and longed to be on the deck breathing fresh air again.

I spent the two-week Pacific crossing crawling around in the slime in the bilges with a droplight as the only illumination. Coffee breaks and meals were the only relief from the drudgery, when I would come up out of my hellhole and join bull sessions with my shipmates. When I had time, I washed and mended my clothes, darned my socks, and occasionally read. I made a canvas sea bag for myself thinking it would come in handy if I jumped ship again, a persistent thought as the voyage progressed. After being uprooted so many times in my life, I thought I might be ready to settle down. Though I had lost touch with Sachiko, I still had some friends in Kobe, and maybe this time with their help I could find a way to stay in Japan.

When we reached Yokohama, I went ashore with three other crew members. We hired a taxi to drive us to Tokyo. The four of us were dressed in our best “go ashore” clothes, which allowed us to be taken for tourists when we walked into the dining room of the Imperial Hotel and sat down for lunch. No one would have guessed by looking at me that only hours before I had emerged from the slime of the ship’s bilges. All that mattered was our clean appearance and our American money. A dollar went a long way in Japan in 1933, so we lived it up on our meager pay until it was time to return to the ship. That night we sailed for Kobe and arrived the following morning.

When our work was finished that day, all hands were granted shore leave, and I went straight to Achi Cameron’s home. I was greeted at the front door by his mother, who ushered me into the dining room. Achi and a group of his young friends were seated around a table. They were mostly expatriates, including a beautiful White Russian named Dusa. We spent the afternoon eating, drinking, and exchanging stories. Achi and the others were mystified by the tales I told of poverty and homelessness in America. Those grim realities seemed faraway. By the time we said our goodbyes that day, I had decided against jumping ship. The prospect of being deported again was daunting, and I finally had to admit to myself that the idea of my finding a home in Japan had been an impractical fantasy.

I returned to the lower depths of my hell-ship and resigned myself to my fate. After visiting the ports of Shanghai and Hong Kong, we were scheduled to sail to Manila. Once we were underway, I felt some abdominal pain and reported to the ship's doctor, looking for any excuse to get out of work. I was actually relieved when he informed me that I had appendicitis and would need to be hospitalized when we arrived in Manila. As soon as we docked, an ambulance delivered me to St. Paul's Hospital in the old Walled City.

Although St. Paul's was classified as a U.S. Marine hospital, most of the nurses were Catholic nuns, and masses were held in a chapel on the main floor. During my admission I was asked what my religion was, and I said I was Catholic though I hadn't been to mass for more than two years. After I was assigned a bed, a male Filipino nurse prepared me for my appendectomy. He shaved my pubic hair while joking in English about the sex change that would result if his razor slipped. While I waited to be taken into surgery, he taught me some Tagalog. I was able to say *mabuhay,* a greeting similar to the Hawaiian word *aloha.*

The operation was performed by a young Texan, Dr. Nance of the U.S. Public Health Service. After a week of lying on my back and being well cared for as a merchant seaman at government expense, I was allowed to get out of bed and sit in a chair. Shortly thereafter, I was approached by one of the nuns who said she had an important matter to discuss with me. I was surprised when she suggested that now might be a good time for me to go to confession and receive communion. Without giving it much thought, I acquiesced and she promised to make the arrangements. An elderly Catholic priest soon appeared and placed a screen around my bed for privacy. He introduced himself, then sat in a chair facing me and began the familiar ritual.

I was already beginning to question my faith, and I shared my concerns with the priest. Since I had first shipped out of San Francisco in 1931, the accumulation of experiences on board ship and ashore had disillusioned me. I felt that life had treated me rather badly, and yet I was not a bad person. I always tried to be fair and do my best despite the hardships. Why should I feel guilty or blame myself for things? What sins had I committed? I finally told the priest that I had nothing to confess. But he challenged me, saying, "You must have had sexual relations with some of those women in those foreign ports."

"Yes, of course," I admitted, "but I don't see anything wrong with that."

"Well, you know, that's a sin, my son."

"Maybe to you, Father, but not to me."

"Well, bless you, anyway, my son. You can receive Holy Communion in the morning."

He granted me absolution and departed, no doubt thinking that he had saved one more soul. But I laid awake most of that night thinking of my days as an alter boy and how my Catholic teachers had always discouraged any serious questioning about issues like the Holy Trinity or the Creation. They insisted these were Divine Mysteries that simply had to be taken on faith.

By the time the nun arrived the next morning with a wheelchair to wheel me down to the chapel, I had decided the time had come for me to stop believing in fairy tales. I told her, "I'm sorry, Sister. I don't mean to offend you, but I've changed my mind. I'm not going." She begged me to reconsider but I was unshakeable in my new conviction. The more she pleaded, the more convinced I was that I had made the right decision. Released from the emotional burden of a faith that was fraudulent on my part, I felt liberated. Having renounced religion at the age of eighteen year, I knew what I didn't believe, even if this act of reason and conscience on my part didn't yet tell me what I did believe.

After my stitches were removed, I was able to travel about the floor in a wheelchair, and I became acquainted with other patients, some of whom were in the venereal ward. One of them was a merchant seaman from a ship that was long gone from Manila. I sometimes found him leaning out the window and talking to an attractive Filipino girl who stood on the sidewalk below. She was a Moro from the island of Mindanao who had recently moved to Manila with the help of this sailor. One day after I was walking again, he called me over to the window and introduced me to the girl. He asked if I would like to take her for a ride in a *karamada*, a horse-drawn carriage. I immediately applied for a pass to get away from the hospital for the rest of the day.

That same afternoon my new friend and I rode through the streets of the old Walled City. It didn't take us long to get acquainted in ways that my unsuspecting sailor friend never intended. He had imagined that she was his private property and would remain loyal until he was released from the hospital. But she and I ended up that night in her bed. It wasn't until early the next morning that I slipped back into the hospital.

After a month in St. Paul's, I was released and informed that I was to return to San Francisco on a Dollar Line ship as a workaway. Since it would be at least two weeks before the next company ship arrived, I was sent to live at an Army and Navy YMCA. I spent those two weeks with my Moro girlfriend. I learned that she had recently fled Mindanao to escape the religious and cultural restrictions of that Moslem stronghold. I admired her for having made such a courageous decision that would surely affect the rest of her life. Though our backgrounds were entirely different, we discovered that we shared much in common. We spent many blissful days together, swimming in the shark-infested waters at Legaspi Landing, sailing in a *banka* (an outrigger canoe with a "leg of mutton" rig), and visiting her friends who lived in thatched houses high above the ground in the jungle. They shared what little food they had with us. When the time came for me to sign on the *SS President Lincoln,* it wasn't easy to say goodbye -- *Mabuhay.* We both knew that it was unlikely we would ever see each other again, and we never did.

I returned via Hong Kong, Shanghai, Kobe, Yokohama, and Honolulu, but there was little I could do on a penny. I was unable to make contact with any of my friends, though I learned that Achi had taken a job on one of the Dollar Line ships. Back in San Francisco in the summer of 1933, I decided to visit family and friends in Red Bluff. I had been away for six years and wondered if I would be welcome in my hometown, knowing that I would be homeless and jobless when I arrived.

I made the trip with my friend Jimmy Stuart who was always looking for adventure. We drove the two hundred miles north in his old jalopy. Our first stop was the jewelry store on Main Street to say hello to George Wilkins, my mother's first cousin by marriage. That night we enjoyed a home-cooked meal and slept in comfortable beds at the Wilkins' home. The following day we spent the afternoon at Dibble Creek, a swimming hole on the Sacramento River. Then Jimmy took off again for San Francisco.

There still remained the questions of how I was to earn a living and what my practical goals in life were. I was welcome to stay with the Wilkins family as long as it might take to get on my feet, and they made sure I had three square meals a day. I learned how to drive a Model T and spent the rest of the summer picking peaches, pumping gas, chasing local skirts and drinking home brewed beer and wine. Those months were the happiest of my life up until that time. I was somewhat unique in the town because most of my friends and former schoolmates had never been far from home. I became something of a local oracle of worldly knowledge for my male contemporaries.

Later that summer, most of my friends, were making plans for the future. Some of the more fortunate ones were going to college, while others were leaving town to look for work. I was lucky to have a job at a local gas station, but I knew it was a dead end. I wrote to an aviation school for information on their pilot training program, but I had to give up the idea because I couldn't afford the tuition. When I heard that one of Franklin Roosevelt's New Deal programs, the Civilian Conservation Corps (CCC), was starting a camp in Lassen National Park, I quit pumping gas and joined the CCC.

The camp was located in a pine forest on the western slope of Mount Lassen, an active volcano about fifty miles east of town. I moved into a military-style barracks with about a hundred young men like myself. We were issued GI khaki work clothes, blankets, and rain gear. The atmosphere was similar to boot camp, but instead of guns we had picks, shovels, axes, and saws. Our job was to cut fire trails to prevent the spread of forest fires that often occurred during the summer months. Fires in the nearby mountains generated so much heat in the valley that we often felt as if we were trapped inside an oven, with the temperature rising as high as 125 degrees.

Among the friends I made that summer were Bob Dagley from Lincoln, Nebraska, and Manuel Ortiz and Enrique Aguirre from Los Angeles. Aguirre was a professional welterweight boxer. To break the monotony in the evenings, Aguirre organized boxing matches. He set up a training program for anyone interested in the fine points of boxing, and I jumped at the chance. After a few weeks of his coaching, which included working out on the punching bag, I was ready for my first fight. My opponent was my friend Bob Dagley, a lightweight like myself. We agreed beforehand not to hit each other too hard. I remember being carried away by the excitement in the ring and landing a left hook on Bob's jaw. Seeing him wince, I immediately regretted that punch, but our three-round bout ended in a draw, and we remained friends.

The boxing matches provided a welcome break from the daily routine of working, eating and sleeping. We were free to leave the camp on weekends, and on Saturday nights we would climb into the back of an army truck to be driven down the mountain into town, usually ending up at an open-air dance hall called the Showboat on the bank of the Sacramento River. A local teenage jazz orchestra played the latest hit tunes. I can still remember the words of such golden oldies as "Learn to Croon" and "Under a Blanket of Blue."

The showboat was popular spot for meeting girls, though guys usually outnumbered the fair sex by about ten to one. The competition turned violent one night when some of the local good-old-boys made the mistake of ganging up on Aguirre. As a Mexican-American, he was considered a "greaser," and he happened to be dancing with one of the hometown girls. When the locals set upon him, he laid some of them out cold and sent others running with black eyes and bloody noses. Like myself, the majority of the young crowd cheered him for defending himself so handily against the bigoted troublemakers.

Most Saturday nights, after dancing and drowning our frustrations in alcohol, we would climb back into the army trucks to return to camp for another week of grueling physical labor. I remember one Sunday morning after a night of carousing, I had stayed out and was sitting on the curb outside a saloon on Main Street, half-asleep and suffering from a hangover. Prohibition has just been repealed. I heard someone say, "Is that you, Georgie?" When I looked up, I was surprised to see Clyde Shaw, my grandmother's old friend. I got up and shook hands, feeling awkward and embarrassed about my present condition. But Clyde clapped an arm over my shoulder and invited me into the saloon for a beer.

After we went inside, Clyde did most of the talking. He told me that after my grandmother died he had married and was now raising a family somewhere east of town. He asked after brother and my father, and I tried to catch him up on the past six years. I told him about my dropping out of high school, shipping out, riding the rails and panhandling. With obvious concern for my welfare, he asked what was to become of me, and I felt ashamed that I had not yet made anything of my life. After we said our goodbyes, I never saw Clyde again. But as a result of the encounter, I decided there was no future for me in Red Bluff and made up my mind to leave as soon as possible.

We weren't supposed to quit the CCC until we completed our tour of duty. But I was determined and Bob Dagley was also ready for a change. After the New Year, we decided to make our getaway. We rode into town with the rest of the gang on a Friday night. As usual, I was traveling "schooner-rigged" with everything I owned in a brown paper bag—toothbrush, shaving gear, and a change of underwear and socks. By the time the army transport trucks showed up for our return, we were already on an all-night ride on the Southern Pacific Railroad.

In San Francisco, we hopped on a Market Street Railway trolley car and made a beeline for the Richmond district, where Bob had a cousin who had agreed to put us up. A week later Bob landed a steady job with a small printing company, and we moved into a skid-row hotel near Third and Howard Streets. We shared a bleak little room with a double bed and nothing more. The shower and toilet were down the hall. I figured the place would do temporarily. By this time, I was resigned to the idea that everything, including life itself, was temporary.

Back in my home port and anxious to start paying my own way, I realized that I could qualify for a higher salary, $45 a month, by upgrading my papers to Able-Bodied Seaman. I had more than enough sea time to meet the one-year requirement, so all I had to do was pass a government test to get my AB certificate. The test included boxing the compass, identifying navigation lights and signals, and demonstrating my knowledge of knots and splices. For me the test was a cinch thanks to my training as a cadet. I passed, acquired my AB ticket, and faced the problem of finding a job once again.

Looking for a ship in the winter and spring of 1934 still meant shaping up at Fink Hall. It would be another few months before the seamen's unions would gain control of hiring. I shaped up again and shipped out as an AB on the *SS West Camargo* of the Pacific, Argentine, Brazil Line. In March I signed on, bound first for British Columbia and then to the east coast of South America. My experience on this ship was to be a crucial turning point in my life that began with my joining the Sailor's Union of the Pacific (SUP) at the urging of the bo's'n and my watchmates. This was the first in a chain of events during the next nine months that were to be an eye-opening education for me.

The SUP, along with the Marine Firemen, Oilers, and Watertenders and the Marine Cooks and Stewards, had begun an organizing drive on the Pacific Coast. At the same time, the rank and file within the International Longshoremen's Association (ILA) had begun to organize a movement under the leadership of an Australian-American dock worker named Harry Bridges. For years, the corrupt officials of these unions, suspected by many of taking bribes from shipowners (a fact later confirmed), had done little or nothing to improve the miserable lot of the seamen and longshoremen. But the rank and file were becoming more militant. The Marine Workers' Industrial Union (MWIU), a left-wing group under Communist leadership, was also beginning to make waves nationwide, forcing corrupt union officials to at least give the appearance of defending our interests.

Soon after we tied up at the dock in Tacoma, Washington, a couple of MWIU organizers found their way aboard and began passing out literature. One of them made a stirring speech while standing on a bench in the sailors' fo'c'sle. My shipmates and I were eager to listen even though he represented a rival union. He was saying what we all wanted to hear -- organize to defend our common interests as working men. He invited all of us to a meeting that night. Because we were only in port overnight, few of us went to the meeting, but he made a lasting impression. As for me, I went ashore and wound up in bed with a blonde professional lady of the night for the going rate of two dollars. Distracted as I was by the pleasure of moment, it didn't occur to me that only fifteen years earlier I had been waving my little American flag from a hotel window just a few doors away.

Our next port of call was New Westminster, British Columbia, where we took on a deck load of lumber. In the evening, after we were secure fore and aft, the whole deck gang went ashore. On the town's main street, we came across a rundown movie theater showing a Soviet film called "The Road to Life." Since there wasn't much else to do in town, some of us decided to see the movie. The film told the story of a group of homeless boys who were living by their wits, begging, riding the rails and looking for work, just as I had done. As displaced victims of World War I and the Russian Revolution, they were now being rehabilitated through counseling and job training under the new Soviet government. Some of the guys scoffed saying this movie was just Communist propaganda, but I was deeply moved by the story.

Heading back south along the Pacific Coast, we made a brief stop at San Pedro for bunkers and fresh water, then went on to Panama and through the canal to San Juan, Puerto Rico. Among the many beer joints, cabarets and whorehouses frequented by sailors in San Juan was a place called the Borinquen Bar. There I met a local girl who took me to her sad little one-room home on a side street in the *barrio* where we spent the night together. This was a familiar episode in the life of a sailor, a pattern that was repeated in one port after another. Having a girl in every port was not quite accurate for us seafaring men because the girl was never really ours. There were exceptions, but usually there was a lack of fidelity on both sides. Without the darker threat of AIDS, safe sex was not practiced by most of us back in those days. The price for such liaisons was sooner or later ending up in the venereal ward in a U.S. Marine Hospital.

From San Juan, my ship went on to Barbados, Rio de Janeiro,

Montevideo, and Buenos Aires. After leaving Argentina, we were heading north for Bahia, Brazil when we heard the first news reports of the 1934 West Coast maritime strike from our radio operator. All of us sailors were anxious to get back to join the strike, and after taking on a load of Brazil nuts in Belem, we reached the dock in San Pedro, California on July 11, 1934.

Scabs, finks, and strikebreakers came crawling aboard the ship like rats to take over the jobs of the striking longshoremen. Under the protection of the local police, these unskilled victims of the Depression began uncovering the hatches, carefully avoiding eye contact with the ship's crew. The way they were dressed told the story of their desperation. Instead of dungarees and hickory shirts, many wore old suits that looked as if they had been slept in for months. There were a few old, beat-up felt hats and what once had passed as dress shoes. These scabs appeared somewhat bewildered by the unfamiliar surroundings and apprehensive about what to expect from us. My gut reaction was a mixture of disgust and anger. They were here to steal our jobs. I regarded them as my enemies and wanted to throw them over the side. But some of the more mature guys in the crew explained to me that these despicable characters were just pathetic tools of the real enemy, the shipowners. What we needed to do was strike the ship immediately.

I had never been on strike before and didn't know what to expect. After notifying the skipper, we packed our sea bags and headed straight for the SUP hall. There we learned that not only was the strike solidly supported up and down the coast, a general strike was in progress in San Francisco. The next morning after being paid off, six of us decided to head back north to our home port. We hired a limousine to drive us the four hundred and fifty miles to San Francisco. We all chipped in and paid what was then a considerable sum of money—ten dollars each. There was barely enough room for the whole gang, with our sea bags and other odds and ends, but somehow we managed. The chauffeur dropped us off on the Embarcadero near the union hall on Clay Street. We checked in, collected our picket cards, and then went off in different directions to find places to stay.

I saw machine guns in place in front of some of the piers and armored vehicles patrolling the waterfront. The Governor had called out the National Guard in response to a series of violent incidents. The two most serious incidents had taken place a week earlier. The first was a cold-blooded murder of four strikers by the police. Small groups of union men had congregated on street corners near the longshoremen's hall when an unmarked police car drove up and stopped in the middle of the intersection. Several plainclothes cops got out of the car and fired point blank into the groups of men. They got back into the car and drove away, leaving four dying men on the sidewalk. The police department later denied having any role in the murders.

A second incident took place on what was later called "Bloody Thursday," July 5, 1934. A battle erupted between strikers and scab-herders who were trying to drive a load of strikebreakers under police protection through the picket line. The strikers stood firm and were winning the battle until the police opened fire. The picketers then retreated toward Rincon Hill; the police followed and continued firing on the unarmed men. Several hundred were injured, and many were hospitalized with gunshot wounds. The Pacific Steamship Owners Association intended to break the strike using every means at their disposal, and the San Francisco Police Department was cooperating with their plan.

But the shipowners and the police underestimated the power of organized labor. The first response to these attacks was a mass funeral march behind the bodies of the murdered longshoremen. This solemn march by many thousands of strikers and sympathizers extended along Market Street from the Ferry Building to the Civic Center. On that day there wasn't a single cop in sight. The workers took over the city, and peaceful order was maintained by sergeants-at-arms of the Joint Strike Committee. It was an inspiring demonstration of working-class solidarity. Every trade union in the city declared a sympathy strike in support of the maritime workers. The city came to a dead stop, and nothing moved for nearly a week.

Most outsiders couldn't understand what all the trouble was about in San Francisco. They were unaware of what it was like for seamen working sixteen hours a day without overtime pay, living in overcrowded, bug-infested quarters, and eating slop that wasn't fit for pigs -- all for thirty to forty dollars a month. There was little public awareness of the vicious shape-up hiring system on the waterfront and the company goon squads.

The waterfront was at a standstill when the unions and shipowners were forced to submit to compulsory arbitration. At about that time I moved in with Bob Dagley, who still had a job with the printing company. I spent the next couple of months on the beach in San Francisco and managed to get by thanks to Bob. My payoff from the *SS West Camargo* was just about gone, so I needed to earn some money to tide me over. Since I had last shipped out, Fink Hall had closed and the unions had flying squads patrolling the waterfront to discourage any shipping off the end of the dock while awaiting the decision of the arbitration board.

One of our demands during the strike was to implement a union-controlled rotary hiring system. Determined to eliminate the shipowners' stranglehold on hiring, the union issued dated shipping cards to all its members on a first-come, first-served basis. The new system was entirely fair, but I found myself near the end of the waiting line.

One afternoon during my waiting period, I was walking along Market Street and bumped into my father. We hadn't seen each other for three years. His first remark was, "I hope you're not mixed up with those strikers." I dodged his question, and he said, "When was the last time you went to communion?" What could I possibly say to this Victorian gentleman who now seemed so out of touch with reality? We stood on the sidewalk and fumbled for words. He made no mention of my brother, probably thinking that I would be a bad influence. Digging down in his pocket, he pulled out his bankroll and gave me some pocket change, evidently embarrassed to admit that he too was down and out. Then without giving me his address or phone number, he walked out of my life for another eleven years.

After putting in a brief stint driving a limousine, I threw my card in at the SUP hall for a job on the *SS Forbes Hauptmann* and shipped out again in October of 1934. The unions had won control of hiring, wage increases, and time and a half for overtime. I now had one of the oldest cards in the hall, so I earned $52.50 a month sailing to Baltimore, Maryland. That trip through the Panama Canal to the East Coast was yet another step in my coming of age politically. Like me, the other crew members were veterans of the strike, and some were more radical MWIU members. I listened closely to them during our bull sessions. Class warfare and revolution were now being openly discussed and my informal education continued after we docked in New York.

I moved into the Seamen's Church Institute on South Street, the cheapest accommodations that I could find, known on the waterfront as the Doghouse. A Federal Relief program for unemployed seamen helped pay for my room and board. The Institute was a block away from the MWIU hall, and most days at noontime outside the front doors there was a street-corner meeting with a soapbox speaker. Sailors based on the eastern seaboard were urged to follow the example set by the unions on the West Coast, where the Maritime Federation of the Pacific had united seamen, teamsters, longshoremen and warehousemen under one powerful umbrella.

I was convinced enough by these rousing speeches to join the MWIU. I didn't know at the time that the union leadership had recently decided at a national convention to disband, advising members to join the various craft union branches of the International Seamen's Union (ISU). The idea was to establish rank-and-file control and to throw out the corrupt union leadership once and for all. I learned about this new strategy later when I approached the National Secretary of the MWIU, Roy Hudson. He said, "Whitey, hang onto your SUP book." Then he suggested, "I have an even better idea. Stay in New York, transfer your book to the Eastern and Gulf Sailors' Association, ISU, and help us organize a rank-and-file movement."

I said excitedly, "When do we start?"

Hudson was encouraging and introduced me to several MWIU members who had recently joined the ISU. One of them was a young seaman from San Francisco named Earl Payne. Like me he was an ex-Catholic, having dropped out from a Jesuit seminary where he had been studying for the priesthood. Earl was an intense guy who had a way of looking me in the eye when he spoke with his eyes constantly darting back and forth searching for a reaction to his words. He gave me a a copy of the *Commu-*

nist Manifesto and invited me to attend a meeting of the Young Communist League (YCL). This was my first exposure to the writings of Karl Marx, and his words were just what I needed to hear: "Workers of the world unite! You have nothing to lose but your chains!" The ethical message was simple and clear in the context of those times, what seemed a matter of common sense then and now, even if with today's complexities we might want to broaden Marx's prescription along the lines, "People of the world unite! You have nothing to lose but all life on the planet!"

I soon joined the waterfront unit of the YCL and worked on the publication and distribution of the first issue of the *ISU Rank and File Pilot.* I regularly attended meetings and helped man the picket lines. Later that year I made a short trip on the *SS San Jacinto*, devoted myself to the revolutionary gospel of Marx and Lenin, met a girl named Margie, learned about lox and bagels and cold borscht with sour cream, read the *Doghouse News,* ate in the Automat, sang the "Internationale," and rode the subway for a nickel. All the while I was making a gradual transition to an activist lifestyle. Working for what I saw as the common good and a more humane world, I had at last found a constructive set of values to replace the religious dogma with which I had grown up.

During the winter of 1935, I continued work on publishing and distributing the *Pilot* on the waterfront. Such activities were producing results. At the monthly union meetings, we would come in with our own militant agenda and take over with support from the rank and file. The labor fakers who presided over these meetings were threatened by our presence. Sometimes, unable to intimidate us or shout us down, they would just say, "This meeting is adjourned," and scurry out with the books. But after another year, we managed to dislodge these piecards from their thrones.

In April, the YCL sent me to Camp Wahchikah in upstate New York for a month-long leadership training program. I was part of a group of young people from both working-class and academic backgrounds. We lived a communal lifestyle, sharing sleeping quarters, eating together in a large dining room, and taking turns with domestic labor. Each day we attended lectures given by union leaders, college professors, writers and artists. One Communist Party functionary by the name of Jack Stachel led a workshop on Marxist-Leninist theory and the history of the trade union movement in the U.S. and overseas. With Stachel, we discussed the rise of Fascism in Europe and the beginning of the anti-Fascist Popular Front movement. My participation in these discussions started to make me aware of the ongoing struggle of the left in Spain and influenced my thinking in the years to come.

In New York City on May 1, 1935, I marched in my first May Day parade. An enormous crowd assembled between Seventh Avenue and Broadway from 34th Street to 23rd Street. Various unions and political groups marched to Broadway and then down to Union Square. Among those represented were transport workers, fur workers, ladies garment workers, Amalgamated Clothing workers, hotel and restaurant workers, hospital employees, artists and writers, machinists, electrical workers, and various fraternal organizations. Socialist and Communist Party contingents unfurled their red banners. The maritime unions did not participate that year on the East Coast, but the following year that would change thanks to our rank and file organizing activities. By the end of 1936 both the Eastern Seaboard and Gulf Coast seamen's unions would catch up with their West Coast brothers.

The dedicated activists who I worked with in the ISU rank and file movement included among others Tommy Ray, Jim Harris, Rudy Patzert, Al Richmond, John Robinson, Paddy Whelan, “Fog Horn” Russel, “Scotty” Edwards, Marty Garnier, Blackie Meyers, Ferdinand Smith, Howard McKenzie, Bill Bailey, Stanley Postek, Smitty Hopkins, Jack Lawrenson, Jimmy Gavin, John MacElroy, and Willi Wilchausen. Quite a few of these organizers would eventually volunteer in Spain.

Having undergone basic training in tactics and strategy of the class struggle, I was anxious to put theory into practice. In early May I went back to sea intending to organize aboard ship, but my plan had to be postponed temporarily. I signed on the *SS American Cardinal* bound for New Orleans and the West Coast. Our first destination was Port Sulphur, Louisiana on the Mississippi River. After we tied up, we began loading a cargo of sulphur. I remember the air that day filled with noxious yellow clouds of sulphur dust. Conditions became all the more unbearable toward sundown with the arrival of swarming black clouds of giant mosquitoes. In the sailors' fo'c'sle, without screens or insect repellent, we were completely at the mercy of these bloodsuckers. By midnight, I was covered with angry red welts and ready to jump over the side. The next morning I packed my gear and demanded to be paid off. I soon found myself on the highway hitching west, then changed my mind and headed into New Orleans.

For the next five months, I lived in the old French Quarter near the corner of Chartres and Dumaine Streets. I shared a large single room on the third floor with “Red” Drummond, the local representative of the Rank and File Committee. There were no facilities or utilities, not even electricity. The room contained two army cots, a table, a couple of chairs, a typewriter, and a carbide lamp. On a floor below, the shower consisted of a tin can with holes poked in the bottom and secured to the end of a cold water pipe.

Soon after I arrived, Drummond shipped out and left me in charge of his union duties. I was responsible for publishing an eight-page monthly bulletin called the *ISU Guide,* the Gulf Coast supplement to the *Pilot.* This was a tough assignment for a hunt-and-peck typist like me, but I managed with the help of another sailor on the beach, Roy "Red" Mouton, who became a lifelong friend. During this period, I received $30 a month from the Rank and File Committee headquarters in New York to cover my expenses. I spent half of that on a monthly meal ticket at a short-order lunch counter called Joe's Lighthouse Restaurant. I also received an occasional "piece off," which was a small monetary gift bestowed by former shipmates, friends, or supporters in the crews of ships that were passing through.

A native Cajun, Red Mouton knew every inch of New Orleans, and together we distributed the *Guide* to every ship that came into port. We also stirred up plenty of heated discussion at the monthly union meetings. I remember one meeting when the port agent, Charlie Thorsen, stood up glaring at the membership and shouted, "If there are any Commies in this hall, why don't you have the guts to stand up and show your faces?" No one was foolish enough to accept the challenge because Thorsen had a goon squad standing by to set upon activist troublemakers like us. But the days of the goon squad were numbered as more and more seamen began to openly support the rank-and-file program, both on board ship and ashore. When it came to rough stuff, we later had ample protection provided by our seafaring comrade Stanley Postek, a professional boxer who also sold macramé to the tourists.

By the time I was ready to ship out again, I had produced four issues of the *Guide,* reprinting articles from the *Pacific Coast Voice of the Federation* as well as writing original pieces, typing stencils and running them off on an ancient mimeograph machine in the local Communist Party headquarters -- all a labor of love, and yet I missed my life on the sea. In October I asked the Committee in New York to send someone to relieve me. After my replacement showed up, I signed on as AB on the *SS Naeco,* an oil tanker on a regular run between the Gulf and the East Coast.

She was my first tanker, quite a different experience than sailing on freighters and passenger ships. Loading and discharging usually took no more than a single day, so we had to make the most the time we had in ports like Houston, Baltimore, Philadelphia, and Fall River, Massachusetts. My shipmates were all solid supporters of the rank-and-file movement. For two and a half months we carried our dangerous cargos of fuel oil, kerosene, or gasoline from the Gulf to the Atlantic coastal ports without incident, though a hurricane we ran into off Cape Hatteras threatened to capsize us in forty-foot seas. We had to hang on to keep from going over the side. But we came through and I learned more than I ever wanted to know twisting valves and cleaning up oil spills. I was paid off in Fall River on January 14, 1936 and took a bus to New York, once again planning to return to union organizing and political activism.

During my eight-month absence from the New York waterfront, two merchant seamen, both militant rank-and-filers, had made a bit of history by drawing public attention to the rising threat of Fascism. The first was Lawrence Simpson, a crew member from the *SS Manhattan* who was arrested in Hamburg, Germany for possession of anti-Nazi literature. Hitler's storm troopers came aboard his ship, ransacked his locker, and took him prisoner. The captain of the *Manhattan*, an American passenger ship, gave them permission to search Simpson's locker and failed to protest against this violation of international law.

A second incident took place in New York on the *SS Bremen,* a German passenger liner with an all-German crew. While the ship was moored in the Hudson off Manhattan's Upper West Side, a band of American seamen led by Bill Bailey, managed to steal aboard shortly before sailing time. After mingling briefly with the passengers, the seamen made a rush for the bow where a Nazi swastika was flying from the jackstaff. Bailey cut the hated rag down and threw it overboard before any Nazi thugs could reach him. Back onshore these courageous sailors were given a rousing welcome by a large crowd of anti-Fascist supporters.

Their story made headlines in some newspapers but was buried in the back pages of others. At the time, the facts about Fascism were widely suppressed in both the U.S. and European democracies, Great Britain and France. A right wing radio priest, Father Coughlin and similar characters around the country had the backing of powerful financial interests sympathetic to Fascism. Even fair-minded liberals underestimated the dangers represented by Hitler and Mussolini. The media's distortions and our government's official policies led to a global tragedy that was first played out in Spain.

In February 1936, the Spanish Fascists were defeated at the polls by the Popular Front and began a campaign of sabotage and terrorism. This was the beginning of three years of bloodshed and suffering for the Spanish people. Not only was the civil war a rebellion against the legitimate Republican government, it was also an invasion. In July 1936, the rebel generals, Franco, Mola, Cabanellas and Queipo de Llano launched their revolt with massive military support from Hitler and Mussolini. By November, Hitler's air force under Hermann Goering's command was bombing Madrid. Our country turned its back on the Republic and placed an embargo on arms shipments to both sides. This official policy known as "non-intervention" played into the hands of Franco and his Fascist allies under the guise of neutrality. The Republic's ability to equip its military forces was limited primarily to arms supplied by the Soviet Union.

I followed the events in Spain closely reading both the straight press and Communist Party literature. During the same period, a sit-down strike took place in San Pedro, California that marked another turning point in maritime union history. The East Coast crew of the *SS California* staged the protest to demand wages and working conditions that matched those of their West Coast union brothers. Secretary of Labor Frances Perkins prevailed upon the crew to bring the ship back to New York. The seamen agreed on condition that their demands would be given serious consideration. On arrival in New York, the bo's'n, Joseph Curran, and some sixty-odd members of the crew were fired and blacklisted. This collusion between the government and the shipowners precipitated a three month national strike, which was immediately declared illegal by ISU officials.

The ISU membership on practically every ship along the East Coast and Gulf came out in support of the crew of the *California.* They responded to the strike call of the Rank and File Committee, which adopted the new name Seamen's Defense Committee. This action, which became known as the Spring Strike, sounded the death knell for the corrupt ISU officials. It was the end of an era for these old-style labor fakers and a new beginning for the men who sailed the ships. When the strike ended in late May, nearly the entire ISU membership supported the Seamen's Defense Committee. The Committee would form the nucleus of what would later become the National Maritime Union, CIO.

I spent the summer of 1936 on the beach in New York City as a waterfront organizer. I lived in a furnished room on 23rd Street as a guest of the New York City Home Relief Bureau part of the time. Then I moved into a Chelsea apartment rented by a married couple who were politically active in the waterfront section of the Communist Party. They provided me with a rent-free room to support my work with the Seamen's Defense Committee. Over the summer I met many young people at YCL picnics in the Bronx, at Tibbets Brook Park and City Island. I went swimming in the ocean at Coney Island, rode the Steeplechase, ate hot dogs at Nathan's, saw Margie for the last time, and fell head over heels for beauty named Cyrille. By September I was read to return to sea.

With the help of the Seamen's Defense committee in New York, I took on another AB job on the *SS Pennsylvania* going to the West Coast. We were paid off in San Francisco October 19, 1936 and joined the picket line for three months. On cold nights we huddled around a bonfire on the Embarcadero. I remember Harry Bridges visiting us to discuss the political issues of the day including the civil war in Spain.

Bridges presided over a huge support rally at the Civic Center that featured Isabel Palencia, the Spanish ambassador to Sweden, and other representatives of the Popular Front government. The atmosphere was charged with emotion and everyone in that packed auditorium was moved that night. The delegates told us about the tragedy that was taking place in their country and made an impassioned plea for aid in the form of medical supplies and ambulances. Earlier that year after the electoral victory by the Popular Front, a program of sweeping economic reforms had been undertaken on behalf of the Spanish working class and peasantry. Franco's criminal insurrection was now hellbent on turning back those progressive reforms, and as the world looked on, innocent civilians were being slaughtered by the rebels and Fascist powers.

The delegates also described the volunteers, including Americans, who were forming the International Brigade to fight side by side with the Spanish people to defend their democratic government. I was just one of many in that audience and similar audiences around the country who strongly supported the anti-Fascist struggle of the Spanish workers. As a young union leader, I wanted to set an example for my fellow seamen. Acting out of conscience and passionate outrage at the atrocities that were being committed, I was ready to volunteer to go to Spain.

Chapter Three

Civil War Odyssey / 1936 - 1939

At the beginning of March 1937, I applied for and received a passport that was stamped "Not valid for travel in Spain" in accord with U.S. State Department policy. A few days later, I boarded a Greyhound bus with six other volunteers and headed for New York City. One of them was a longshoreman, Joseph Roscoe Ensign, and the other five were fellow seamen: Norman Dorland, John Bowman, Jack Weiss, Larry O'Toole, and John Rody. A Communist Party committee was outfitting volunteers and seeing to the task of transporting them to France. We reported to the committee's headquarters, which was a loft on Second Avenue at Twelfth Street. We were advised that before entering Spain we would need to travel as inconspicuously as possible under the guise of being tourists.

On March 17th, we embarked from New York as passengers on the *SS President Roosevelt* bound for Le Havre. During the crossing our conversations told me that all of us were deeply committed to this cause and ready to put our lives on the line without equivocation. We took the train to Paris where we were met by "Comrade Jack" of the French Committee to Aid the Spanish People. After a briefing at committee headquarters on the Boulevard de la Villette, we were put up in a small *pension* nearby. We were told that it would be several days before we could continue our journey to Spain. Warned not to discuss our plans with anyone, we were happy to continue our impersonation of carefree sightseers enjoying the good life of Paris.

We were aware before our arrival that official French policy with regard to Spain was non-intervention, including an arms embargo. But we were surprised by the political realities we saw being played out between the vacillating government and the French people, who were overwhelmingly anti-Franco. Although the Socialist-led Front Populaire was in power, there were still pro-Fascist elements in the government preventing aid from going to the Spanish Republic. We learned that some of these friends of Franco had infiltrated the Ministry of the Interior. Under pressure from British and American interests, the French Prime Minister, Leon Blum allowed this to happen despite widespread protests and dissent from inside his coalition government.

During our week in Paris, there was a mass funeral march for Valerian Couturier, led by the Mayor and members of the Chamber of Deputies in their official robes. Valerian Couturier had been the editor of *L'Humanité,* official organ of the French Communist Party. Over one million people from all walks of life marched in that funeral procession. Every organization in the Front Populaire was represented, including Leon Blum's Socialist Party. It was a powerful display of unity in the struggle against Fascism. All of us volunteers wanted to take part, but we were forced to maintain a low profile to protect our cover.

Warned against fraternizing, we were nevertheless a group of young men for whom the charms of Paris in the springtime were irresistibly romantic. With our clandestine adventure set against a backdrop of danger, the war seemed to act as an aphrodisiac, heightening the intensity of the drinking, flirting, and whatever other *divertissements* and sexual encounters took place. The circumstances made this experience entirely different for me than what I had been accustomed to as a sailor on shore leave.

I went to the Left Bank one night with Johnny Rody, Jack Weiss, and one of the other guys in my group. Earlier that afternoon in a five-and-ten-cent store called *Lanoma,* these three had met a “million dollar baby” working behind the counter. This alluring mademoiselle spoke perfect English, and they made a date to meet her that night in a little cabaret. I was invited to tag along, and after dancing away the evening with her and drinking a bottle of champagne, I ended up taking her home. Near the Metro station in Issy Les Moulineaux, we stopped for one last drink in an all-night bistro and watched the sunrise. We walked to the apartment where she lived with her mother and sister, and made a date to meet again.

I saw Odette several times after that. She never pried or questioned me about anything, but she must have suspected that we were all volunteers. When the time came to say our farewells, we were again arm in arm at the Issy Les Moulineaux station. Before we parted, I said, “I think you know where I'm going.” She said softly, “Yes, I do.” We promised to write and stay in touch. *J'attendrai, le jour et la nuit; j'attendrai toujours, tant retour.*

More volunteers had arrived from the States. We were now a group of thirty. An American newspaper correspondent, Evan Shipman was assigned to lead us into Spain. Shipman had lived in France for some years, and in addition to being fluent in the language, he was an avid connoisseur of wine and cuisine. After a briefing at committee headquarters, we took an overnight train to Toulouse. We were put up in a modest *pension* that served delightful French family-style cuisine. Shipman enjoyed his role as tour leader, introducing a motley bunch of seamen and longshoremen to the fine art of French gourmet. Most of my group came from the East Coast, though there were also a couple of expatriate Finns from Canada. We were diverse in terms of education and work experience, bound together only by our shared commitment to fight Fascism.

For several days, we basked in the sunlight of Basque country. We traveled in groups of three and four and took to wearing berets like the natives. The hours dragged by pleasantly but slowly, with a trip across the snow-capped Pyrenees looming ahead of us. Some volunteers feared that after we had come this far, the war might end before we had our chance to take part in the action. But one night our orders finally came through. We were to meet a bus on the outskirts of the city. Only Shipman knew the exact location. We followed him, straggling behind until we found the bus waiting for us in the dark. We climbed on and headed south toward the Pyrenees, which were about an hour's ride from Toulouse.

On Shipman's advice, we tried to get some sleep before our planned all-night hike across the mountains. I was just dozing off when the bus screeched to a halt near the village of Muret. I looked out and saw a police roadblock ahead of us. At first I assumed that it was just a routine check. The driver hastened out and we heard what sounded like polite conversation. Shipman went outside and joined in the discussion. Then a *gendarme* came aboard and walked down the aisle shining a flashlight into our sleepy faces. The driver was ordered to turn the bus around. In less than half an hour we found ourselves back in Toulouse, transported through the gates of a medieval prison with thick stone walls with turrets.

For the next two weeks we were treated as common criminals. We slept on straw mattresses on a cold stone floor. Early in the morning, a prison guard would escort all of us down a spiral staircase to the ground floor and across to a second spiral staircase leading up to our daytime cell. On our way between the two staircases, we walked past a large hand truck piled high with loaves of bread. A prison inmate standing there handed each of us a loaf as we passed by. Once we were safely locked into our daytime cell, there was nothing to do but wait for our daily food ration.

At about ten another trusted prison inmate would arrive outside the cell door with a large cauldron of "soup," which consisted of hot water with a few cabbage leaves floating on the surface. This concoction along with some bread was the extent of the meal served for breakfast, lunch, and dinner. We ate while seated on benches at either side of a long wooden table, surrounded by stone walls and small barred windows. In a far corner at the other end of the room was a large metal tub that served as a latrine. Each day two of us had to carry this stinking mess down into the prison yard and dump its contents into a gutter. This chore was timed to coincide with a daily hour of outdoor calisthenics, which we took seriously.

We had many supporters on the outside who were demanding our release. Because of the mounting pressure on the authorities, our status was changed to the *regime politique*. As political prisoners, we were allowed to buy certain items from the canteen (wine, chocolate, and cigarettes), and we were given cots and blankets. But the bread and "soup" remained our staple diet, and the daily latrine duty continued. As the days dragged on, we had time to get better acquainted. While cut off from news from the outside world, we took part in lively discussions of the history of the Spanish Republic, the rise of Fascism in Europe, dialectical materialism, the Russian Revolution and so forth.

It was bad enough that we were being held prisoners without bail, but the crowning insult came when a U.S. consular official from Bordeaux confiscated our passports. U.S. policies were not only aiding the Fascists but also encouraging persecution of anti-Fascists like ourselves despite the fact that the sympathies of most Americans were on the side of the Republic. At the end of April, the world was shocked when the city of Guernica was destroyed by incendiary bombing, with the attackers making no distinction between military and civilian targets. The bombing was a terrorist operation carried out by aircraft from Hitler's Condor Legion. Pablo Picasso's famous painting not only exposed the horror of the event but also captured the fear of what was to come in a world that had now witnessed weapons of mass destruction for the first time used on civilians.

Protests against our incarceration took place on May 1st both inside and outside the Toulouse prison. We prisoners asked for and were granted permission to organize a May Day celebration. While we regaled with songs and speeches in the prison yard, the citizens of Toulouse held a mass demonstration outside the prison walls calling for our immediate release. That day we learned more about the political reality of our situation. With tears in his eyes, the warden of the prison told us that someone in the Ministry of the Interior had ordered our arrest. He explained that the formal charge against us was "attempted violation of the non-intervention treaty." Upon hearing this news, we sang the "Internationale," with shouts of "*Vive la République Espanola"* coming from outside the prison walls.

A few days later we boarded a police bus early in the morning and headed into Muret to stand trial. I remember a magenta sky at sunrise as we walked along the narrow cobblestone streets toward the courthouse of that ancient village. After being led into the courtroom, we took our seats and waited for the curtain to rise. We were asked to stand as the magistrates entered wearing black robes and wigs. Our lawyer, who was wigless in a black robe, had been retained by *La Depeche,* an influential Socialist newspaper. After the charges against us were read, our lawyer offered a defense argument similar to one that had been made at another trial of a group of American volunteers in March. The defense attorney stated, "There are crimes, and crimes. Theirs is a political crime—that they love liberty, democracy, peace. Before this court, I wish to pay homage to these Americans who left homes, jobs, families, and friends to fight for their ideals. So should every Frenchman honor them, for these ideals of liberty and democracy—are they then foreign to France? I beseech this tribunal to temper justice, the letter of the law, with mercy in this case, for the honor of France and of humanity."

Despite an eloquent defense, we were found guilty as charged, sentenced to forty days in prison, and ordered to leave French territory within eight days after our release. The sentence was retroactive. Since we had already served thirty-five days, we returned to prison for only five more days. In a sense the court ruling was in our favor. We could have been deported on the spot, but instead we were given the necessary time to make plans to complete our mission.

On the morning of our release, we walked out of the prison with our suitcases and returned to our *pension*, where all of us shaved and bathed, put on clean clothes and had our first decent meal in six weeks. The next morning, after *petit déjeuner*, we walked in small groups to the railroad station, where we boarded a train for Marseilles. After arriving, we walked along the station platform to another train waiting to take us north. We stopped over in Arles, Van Gogh's adopted village. We never drank absinthe, but there was always vermouth and plenty of red wine. We stayed five days at a small hotel owned by an Italian couple who had two sons fighting in Spain in the Garibaldi Brigade. I shared rooms upstairs with John Bowman, and we were made to feel like members of the family. At noontime the place filled with workers who came in for café cognac and games of pool. I shot pool with them, and that diversion, along with cards, checkers and reading, was enough to keep us occupied.

We couldn't wander outside during the daylight hours because of the secret police, a danger that our Italian innkeeper knew well. After dark, he would take us out for long walks on the bank of the Rhone River. One Sunday he decided it was safe to take us to a nearby park, where we learned the game of bocci. All went well during our time in Arles, except one night when my fellow volunteer, Larry O'Toole went AWOL. He was criticized and offered up his apologies. Later, his outstanding record of bravery in action more than made up for his lapse in discipline.

On an afternoon in mid-May, we took a train to Marseilles. Across the street from the railroad station was a small café, and there we sat at separate tables in groups of three and four. One by one, the tables emptied as guides appeared, sat for a moment, then left with their designated groups. After a half hour according to plan, I was left waiting alone at my table, sipping a café au lait. I wasn't concerned because I had complete faith in those running the operation. I learned later that many of those working on our behalf in the underground were anti-Fascist Italian refugees.

When it was my turn to leave, I was joined by a tall, dark-haired young man who quietly told me in French that we would first walk a short distance, then take a trolley car. The sun was sinking as we walked together through bustling streets. When we boarded the trolley car, he paid the fare and said something to the conductor. Riding along the waterfront, I had a breathtaking view of the harbor and the ships tied up at the docks. My companion got off at the next stop, saluting me with the clenched fist of the Front Populaire.

I was the only passenger still on the car. At the next stop, the conductor called me to the exit door and pointed outside to a ship flying a red, yellow and purple flag at her stern. It was the flag of the Spanish Republic, and the ship was the *SS Capitan Seguro.* When I stepped down onto the cobblestones, the conductor raised his fist and said softly, *"Salud, camarade."* I returned the salute and headed straight for the ship. As I approached, I was alarmed to see two gendarmes standing watch at the foot of the gangway. But they soon turned their backs and disappeared behind a pile of lumber on the dock. *Voilà!* A perfectly executed plan by the French Committee to Aid the Spanish People.

When I reached the top of the gangway, I was greeted with a warm *"Salud, camarada"* from the Spanish chief mate, who quickly ushered me into the dining salon. There were at least at least two hundred volunteers sitting at tables eating dinner. As I searched the crowd for a familiar face, someone behind me yelled, "Hey, Whitey!" I turned around and saw my gang, safe and sound and in fine spirits. We enjoyed a quiet celebration that night anticipating the last leg of our journey.

"Quiet" was the watchword. We were on board a Spanish ship,

but we were tied up in a French seaport. Because of the non-intervention policy, we were still in considerable danger. For the next thirty-six hours, we kept out of sight, hiding from the French authorities in port. After the ship left Marseilles, we charted a course to try to avoid detection by the naval vessels of the non-intervention patrol. Our ship hugged the Mediterranean coast en route to Spanish territorial waters. We were challenged by the commander of a British destroyer outside the port of Barcelona. He asked the routine questions about our cargo and destination, then allowed us to proceed. We were lucky that it wasn't one of Hitler's or Mussolini's warships. Some volunteers weren't so fortunate. Not long after we sailed, the *SS City of Barcelona* was sunk by an Italian submarine and took heavy losses. Fascist attacks on unarmed merchant vessels were the ongoing reality of the non-intervention policy.

Within hours after arriving in Barcelona, we were on a train speeding south to Valencia, then on to Albacete. At each station stop along the way, we were greeted by friendly crowds wanting to have a look at us and show their support. There were shouts of "Viva los Americanos." Acknowledging our common struggle, peasants working the fields waved and raised clenched fists as the train sped by. We arrived in Albacete just after sunrise and were met by French officers from the État Major, headquarters of the International Brigades. They quickly assembled us into a kind of ragtag military formation and off we marched with our suitcases. Along the way, we met a number of wounded comrades who were being taken to hospitals on the Mediterranean coast. Seeing them and listening to their horror stories from the front made me realize what we were in for. But I thought if these guys had stood the test and at least managed to come out alive, so would I.

During the course of that first day, we were transformed from civilians to uniformed soldiers. In addition to regulation boots, *pantalones*, khaki berets, sweaters, and ponchos, we were each issued a mess kit, canteen and blanket. Late in the afternoon, we left our suitcases and civilian clothes behind and climbed into the backs of army trucks that took us to Tarrazona, the training base for the new Washington Battalion.

Located in the heart of the region known as *La Mancha,* Tarrazona was a little market town surrounded by olive groves and wheat fields. We were quartered in a number of small whitewashed buildings at the edge of town. In each building there were several rooms with double-decker bunks. I shared a room with Joe Young, Gene Wolman, Joe Stone, Vaughn Love, and a guy named Bowers, who always had a sketchpad handy. With all the rooms opening onto courtyards on the street, the sight of goats wandering in and out of the barracks became a source of daily amusement.

Our battalion consisted of three infantry companies and one machine gun company. Each company had three sections, and each section three groups. I was assigned to the 3rd section of the Ist Company, which was composed entirely of merchant seamen. Our company commander was Captain Hans Amlie, brother of a Wisconsin congressman. His adjutant was Lieutenant Phil Detro from Texas. Our section leader was a fellow seaman, Sergeant Wallace Burton, and my group leader was my friend Joe Young from the New York waterfront. He was a corporal, or *cabo*, as it was called. There were also political commissars: Bernard Ades for the Ist Company and John Robinson (Robbie) for our seamen's section.

The training school at Tarrazona was like a western movie set with buildings made of logs. Pine trees sheltered the barracks and classrooms from detection by aircraft. We spent a month learning the basic skills of infantry warfare: marching in single-file battle formation fifteen paces apart, advancing in short rushes, digging foxholes, memorizing strategy and tactics, drilling with weapons and taking target practice. We were each issued a helmet, a rifle, ammunition, and an incredibly ancient type of hand grenade with a short fuse. I now brandished a bolt-action Soviet rifle that had Cyrillic printing and a hammer and sickle on the barrel.

We had time to acquaint ourselves with the village and surrounding countryside. Most of our guys made friends easily with the villagers despite the language barrier. I walked along dusty roads outside of town and saw mules being used to grind wheat and pump water just as they had been doing for centuries. Tied to long poles, the faithful beasts would walk around and around in a circle for hours. One day as several of us were passing a farmhouse, some peasants invited us into their patio to share their olives and wine, which we drank from a *porron.* We later scrounged around the village to find ingredients for the Spanish version of a tortilla -- eggs, onions, sausage and potatoes. A family in town invited us to use their outdoor charcoal fire to prepare this delightful concoction. At a local café we feasted on *churros* (crullers) with *café con leche* (coffee with milk). On some occasions, the whole battalion sat down to dinner in the church for a local delicacy known as "burro stew."

I knew that reports of church burnings in the early days of the war had been distorted by the press back home. The Catholic Church was the largest single landowner in Spain and much of its powerful hierarchy sided with Franco. In some instances, churches became targets for angry peasants who had been exploited for centuries. Under the influence of the Spanish Anarchists, they went on a rampage against the symbols of Catholic authority. Such actions were condemned by the Popular Front and the

Communist Party. Fascist troops often made the churches centers of rebel resistance, fortifying them and putting machine guns in their belfries, then labeled the Republicans “godless Bolsheviks” for attacking them. As far as I could tell, religion was never really a major issue in the war despite efforts by the right wing press to make it appear so.

By the end of our training, we were an effective fighting unit, not the best equipped perhaps, but we more than made up for that with our morale. In contrast to soldiers in an ordinary conscripted army, we regarded ourselves as comrades in a People’s Army. Our discipline was voluntary and founded on our shared commitment to the cause. When orders were given, we were ready to follow them, but we understood that our officers were also comrades. There was a sense of social equality between us. We all at the same food, wore the same basic uniforms, and received the same nominal pay. The kind of bullying and abuse that rank causes in a conscripted army was nowhere to be seen among the volunteers.

On June 15, 1937 we assembled in the village square of Tarrazona de la Mancha and were loaded into a convoy of Russian-made army trucks. We drove in the direction of Madrid, and late that afternoon arrived in the village of Tielmes. After dinner, we settled in for the night. Joe Young and I slept on the ground beside railroad tracks. Shortly after falling asleep, we were awakened by the sound of farting burros and cursing peasants. They kept it up until daybreak, with screams of *¡Arre burro! ¡Me cago en Dios!* Later that day, we moved into a position of “close reserve” outside the village of Morata de Tajuna, where we set up camp in an olive grove.

Close reserve in this case meant that we were a few miles behind the Jarama front lines, where the Lincoln Battalion had played an important role in the defense of Madrid earlier in the year. Now everything was quiet.

Our main activity for the next two weeks was trying to keep our equipment and ourselves dry. Even our pup tents failed to protect us. During heavy downpours, Joe and I were almost washed out of our tent. One afternoon he and I visited a tank corps stationed about a mile away. Getting there in daylight was no problem, but by the time we started back, it was pitch dark and we were hit by a violent thunderstorm. Groping between flashes of lightning, we hurried in the direction of camp without thinking about the irrigation ditches we had easily crossed earlier. I stumbled into one of them and found myself in water up to my armpits. After we made our way back to our tent, I spent the rest of that night shivering, wrapped in an itchy wool blanket.

It was the end of June, and the sun rose early. We packed our gear, filled our canteens, and marched back into Morata. As we entered the plaza, we were met by a cheering crowd of townspeople. A few days earlier we had helped them harvest their wheat in the surrounding fields, and now they wanted to show their gratitude. The ceremony began with a short address by our battalion commander, Mirko Markovicz. Then we listened to a brief farewell speech delivered in Spanish by a representative of the local Popular Front committee. I understood most of what he said, but the feeling of good will came through loud and clear even without a translator.

We climbed aboard the convoy of army trucks and embarked on what amounted to a mystery ride. There was a feeling of excitement in the air as we jounced and rattled over potholed back roads. None of us had the slightest hint of where we were going. The only clue was the position of the sun that told us we were heading north. By late afternoon, we turned west. We had circled northwest of Madrid. By nightfall, we came to a stop at a crossroads on the edge of a blacked-out village. All was quiet as we disembarked in the darkness and lined up to begin marching. *Adios, camiónes.*

We were not alone. As we marched, we passed tanks, artillery, and all kinds of equipment parked on the side of the road. We heard other languages being spoken: French, German, Italian, Polish, and Spanish among others. Occasionally, we stopped for a much-needed five-minute rest. Lying there in a ditch beside the road, I remember a group of Spaniards marching by in their rope-soled shoes, *alpargatas*, singing quietly as they marched, "*Somos comunistas, revolucionários y luchamos todos por la libertad.*" They were part of the Fifth Regiment under the command of Colonel Juan Modesto.

It was obvious that we were moving into an offensive position. To ensure secrecy, we rested in the daytime by taking cover in the trees by the road. On the Fourth of July, we had a small celebration and an especially good meal before taking off for the next all-night march. We spent the following day in a pine forest, where we rested and filled our canteens with water from a cool mountain stream. We were told to remain there and be ready to move out at a moment's notice. The excitement of making it to the front at last vied with the queasy feeling of leaping into the unknown of battle. At daybreak the next day, we were ordered to fall in.

Marching along a dusty road early that morning, we passed the fortress of El Escorial. The landscape descended gently, warming up as the sun climbed higher in the summer sky. We soon left the road and broke up into single-file battle formation. At first all was quiet as we advanced slowly down through ravines and gullies, keeping a few paces apart as we had been trained to do. Suddenly, we heard the unmistakable whooshing sound of artillery shells passing over our heads. I felt a twinge of fear and wondered whether they were ours or theirs. We were soon relieved to learn that it was protective fire to cover our advancing troops. This was the opening barrage of the Brunete offensive.

As soldiers operating on a need-to-know basis, we would only learn later the two-fold objective behind the offensive: to relieve the pressure on Madrid by cutting off the enemy here, and to compel Franco to divert planes, tanks and troops from the north, drawing them away from Asturian and Basque Republican positions. The operation utilized fifty thousand men, including the Lister division, the Modesto division, and all five International Brigades.

After resting briefly in a gully on the safe side of a hill, my group pressed forward again. It was high noon, and the sun and summer heat were already affecting us. We could see the village of Villanueva de la Cañada in the distance shimmering like a mirage, its church tower seemingly suspended in midair. Then suddenly we were under fire. Bullets whistled overhead, and then came the shock of exploding mortar shells that made the earth tremble underfoot. Each black explosive cloud seemed to get closer as the enemy fire intensified. Screams told me that Fascist bullets were finding their marks around me.

I was disoriented and lost contact with my group leader. We were advancing in short rushes across a dried-up river bed. The heat was now so unbearable that I threw away excess equipment and was left with only my helmet, rifle, ammunition, and empty canteen. At one point in the confusion, I stumbled forward and happened upon the mortally wounded body of John Bowman, one of our original group of merchant seamen from San Francisco. Another soldier had already given him first aid and moved him to a spot in the shade, but it was hopeless. His life spilled out red on the ground until there was nothing more anyone could do for him. I watched helplessly as he lay there dying, then carried on, trying to put the terrible image out of my mind.

Our advance stopped for the day just a few yards further. We were pinned down by mortar and machine-gun fire at the bottom of a ravine below Villanueva de la Cañada. At least we were together again, except for the dead and wounded. As we lay on the bank of a ravine, which afforded us some protection, we could hear the crack of explosive bullets hitting the tree branches above our heads. There was little return fire from our outfit. Captain Amlie clambered up the side of the ravine to get a better look at the enemy positions. I saw him fire his rifle several times toward the village.

Trying to follow the captain's example, a couple of the guys went too far up the ravine and got hit. Moe Fishman and 'Old John' Givney were wounded. Old John was carried away on a burro to the first aid station. I don't think I fired my rifle more than half a dozen times that afternoon. When I did, I held the rifle up over the edge of the embankment, pointed it toward the village and pulled the trigger, firing into the no-man's land that stretched between their line and ours. I didn't stick my head up to aim for fear of getting it blown off. Enemy fire was heavy, and we were in a vulnerable position. We knew that we would have to wait for nightfall to make another move. Just before sundown, the Republican air force joined the fray. Engines roared as the planes flew over the village and dropped a deafening string of bombs on the Fascist machine-gun emplacements, including one in the church tower. After the bombing, things quieted down that night. We stayed in place, and somehow I managed to get a few hours of sleep.

The next morning Joe Young and I came across the first dead enemy soldiers on the outskirts of the village, which had been taken by other

International Brigade units during the night. We stopped in a bombed-out machine-gun pill box and looked at the gory remains of several young blond soldiers. The sight would stay with me the rest of my life. They wore the dark uniforms of the Nazi Condor Legion. Their bodies were blown wide open so their internal organs were exposed to the blazing hot sun. Twenty-four hours earlier, I had watched John Bowman gasping for his last breath. Now we were looking at what was left of his killers. I thought of how these horribly mutilated remains were once children cradled in the arms of loving mothers. Now it was necessary to kill what they had become. There was never any doubt in my mind about that. They had allowed themselves to become the instruments of Fascism, and now they were its victims.

Joe and I were left behind that night. The entire battalion went ahead without us before daybreak while we were hidden in a thicket, fast asleep. Villanueva had been captured, and the road to Brunete was filled with men and equipment. We had to find our outfit, which we could only guess was somewhere up ahead. Before leaving the village, which was now deserted, we decided to search the ruins of the bombed-out church. Looking through the rubble, we found a pile of military documents and took them with us to hand over to the battalion staff.

As we hurried along the road to Brunete, we could see the buildings of the village that lay ahead. The road in front of us was empty and strangely quiet. We sensed that something had to be wrong, and soon found out what it was. The sudden whine of bullets told us that Brunete was still in enemy hands. We hit the ground and lay flat, then crawled backwards, inching our way until we were able to get off the road. We scurried down into a dried-up creek bed, and once out of rifle range, we ran along the gully until I couldn't go any further and fell to my knees. The temperature was at least a hundred degrees, and I was exhausted from hunger, thirst and lack of sleep. I dug frantically into the sandy river bed until I was able to drink from a pool of warm, brackish water.

After quenching my thirst, I started off again to look for my unit. I came to a road filled with men and equipment from the Lincoln Battalion. The first person I ran into was Hy Stone, one of three Stone brothers. We stuck together for a while, taking cover in ditches during bombings and strafing from enemy aircraft. A column of our tanks was advancing slowly along the road with us, occasionally firing over our heads. Hy told me he had seen some of the Washingtons and pointed me in their direction. I thanked him and left the road again to look for my outfit.

Operating on pure adrenalin, I ran through gullies and crossed open fields. Eventually, I came upon a group of Spanish soldiers who had taken cover behind a small clump of trees. I didn't know which outfit they were from or who they were. Seeing my state of exhaustion, one of them offered me a drink of water from his canteen, and I gratefully accepted. At that moment, we were startled by an English-speaking officer who came out of nowhere waving his pistol and urging us to move forward. Carrying a riding crop in one hand and a pistol in the other, he was totally nonchalant, as if he were on a Sunday stroll. He fit the description of Lieutenant Edward Cecil Smith, the Canadian commander of our second company who was said to have a "Princess Pat" regimental background. Heeding his orders, we all scrambled to our feet and made our way forward. Enemy fire was more sporadic now. Guns thundered fitfully and there were occasional puffs of black smoke from mortar shells. The random whine of stray bullets was always cause to hit the ground.

I came through unscathed. Things quieted down later in the afternoon, and I finally caught up with Joe Young and the rest of my group. The battalion had advanced to a point overlooking the Guadarama River. In the distance beyond the river, we could see the rocky heights of Mosquito Ridge, a heavily fortified emplacement to which the Fascists had retreated. We knew we would eventually have to storm that ridge, which overlooked the surrounding terrain for miles. It was close to sundown, and the whole battalion was desperately in need of rest, food and water. We were all relieved when the order came to dig in for the night. After we finished digging our foxholes, Joe and I and a few others went looking for water, which we found in a well behind our lines. While we filled our canteens, I was subjected to a tirade of complaints by Bill McCuistion, one volunteer who was always griping about something.

McCuistion was one of those men whose self-serving wrath and self-pity were all-consuming. Such characters were referred to by many as "demoralized elements." When I first met him on the New York waterfront in 1935, he was a militant organizer of the rank-and-file movement in the old ISU. I had worked with him on putting out the first issue of the *Rank and File Pilot.* Over time I realized that he had a serious alcohol problem. In Spain, he wound up in a labor battalion in Albacete, which was the last place I ever saw him. In later years back in the States, he became an informer for the House Un-American Activities Committee. Still later, I heard he had been spotted lying in a gutter dead drunk on West 23rd Street in Manhattan.

Back in my foxhole, I curled up in a fetal position, terrified whenever enemy shells exploded near enough to shake the ground under me. I was lucky not to be on sentry duty. Out of sheer exhaustion, I fell into a fitful asleep. At daybreak we were awakened and told to prepare to advance again. Minutes later, we were charging down a long hill toward our uncertain objective, which was never identified for us, whatever it was. We quickly found ourselves in an exposed position under heavy fire. Scared shitless, we continued in short rushes, at times shouting and singing to keep our spirits up. At the bottom of the hill, we came to another dried-up river bed. We crossed it and then started up the hill on the opposite bank. Stopping for a breather, I saw a woman in uniform holding a wounded Spanish officer in her arms. Struggling for breath, he suddenly cried out "*Ay, madre mía!*" The woman wept quietly with her arms around him until he died moment later.

We dug in at the top of the hill next to the British battalion. Although we were on the safe side of the hill, we were still below Mosquito Crest. The Fascists were able to observe our movements and directed their fire at our position, keeping us pinned down. During the next few days, we tried repeatedly to mount an attack and suffered more losses, mostly from enemy mortar fire. A volunteer called K.O. was killed by a mortar shell, and our company adjutant was wounded. In battle, a minute can seem like a day, and each day becomes an agonizing eternity. The terror goes on ceaselessly, and you begin to wish for any break in the bombing and shelling that would allow you to rest and recover shot nerves. With the smell of death all around us, we were sleepless for days at a time.

One night I was assigned to sentry duty by Sergeant Wallace Burton. I was as exhausted as the rest of my group, and he soon caught me dozing off. I thought at first he was going to shoot me on the spot, but I got off with an angry lecture and managed to stay awake until I was relieved. As soon as I returned to my foxhole, all hell broke loose. Someone started shooting at us, and within a few seconds it sounded like a Fourth of July nightmare. Everyone, including myself, began firing wildly into the blackness in front of our foxholes. The British outfit on our flank did the same. During the excitement, I took refuge in a deeper trench with one of our English comrades. The two of us kept firing, reloading, and firing until a cease-fire order was passed along the line. Afterwards, there were rumors about Fascist raiding parties and Moorish cavalry, but we never actually found out what we had been shooting at.

During that first week of battle, we sometimes went to meetings with our political commissars down in the river bed. The purpose of these meetings was to bolster our morale. Candy bars, cigarettes and mail from back home were passed out. The commissars listened to our complaints, answered questions and tried to reach a democratic solution to any problem. These brief respites from the carnage were mightily appreciated.

On July 12th, because of our heavy casualties, we were given an opportunity to volunteer as stretcher bearers, and I stepped forward. The job was to carry the wounded from the first aid station in the river bed behind our foxholes to the evacuation station five hundred meters away. In order to accomplish this, we had to cross a hillside exposed to enemy fire. Sometimes two men could accomplish the task, depending on the weight of the wounded soldier. We would run with the stretcher for about twenty or thirty meters and then drop to the ground to rest, always looking ahead for cover. Running with the stretcher and being an unarmed moving target was even more terrifying than advancing on the battlefield.

One afternoon, after making several successful trips back and forth to the first aid station, I was asked to carry our battalion adjutant, Captain Trail, who had taken a hit. He weighed over two hundred pounds, and it took four of us to carry him. The poor guy was groaning and begging us to get him to the doctor. The field hospital, from where he was to be evacuated, was nestled among willow trees on the safe side of a hill. It wasn't really a hospital at all, but a collection of wounded men on stretchers. They were tended by medical personnel under the direction of a French doctor. This was the pickup point for our ambulances. As soon as we arrived, I discovered that Captain Trail had been hit again while we were carrying him on the stretcher.

At that moment, I stood staring at his lifeless body and felt sick to the pit of my being. I was soon weeping uncontrollably. Then I started ranting and raving, at times humming a tune called "Madeleine" that I remembered from a Hollywood war movie. Seeing my fit of hysteria, the French doctor tried to snap me out of it with a pep talk in broken English. But the more he tried to help, the more hysterical I became. I had reached the limits of my endurance, and my mind simply cracked under the strain. I could see and hear what was going on around me, but I had no conscious control anymore over what I was doing and saying.

Finally, one of our ambulances pulled up. I recognized the driver. He was one of my old friends from the San Francisco waterfront, Nate Thornton. He took one look at me and said, "C'mon, Whitey. Hop in back and I'll drive you to the base hospital." I climbed inside with several wounded soldiers from other units. During much of our two-hour journey, I continued humming that ridiculous tune. Eventually, I calmed down, and Nate had me sit up front with him.

After we arrived at the hospital and discharged the wounded, Nate went inside and soon returned with blankets and food. We slept on the ground beside the ambulance that night. Early the next morning, one of the nurses brought us coffee and *churros*. Somehow it was decided that

I should be sent to headquarters in Madrid. I said goodbye to Nate and climbed into the front seat of one of our Russian trucks. The driver was a volunteer from New York. After a perilous ride over a winding back road, we arrived in Madrid about two hours later. On a broad tree-lined avenue, we parked in front of a huge government building.

I was directed inside the office of the Political Commissar of the International Brigades, Ralph Bates. In the hallway, I was met by his secretary, a young English-speaking woman who asked me why I was wearing a helmet. In my disarray, I'm sure I was a sorry sight. After explaining to her that I had just come from the front, she took me into the office. Bates was sitting behind a large desk. He had me sit down and questioned me about my condition and what had taken place on the battlefield. After hearing me out, he decided to send me to work in Albacete, the base of the International Brigades.

I was given a *salvoconducto* (safe-conduct pass) for my travels and sent to spend the night in a military barracks. Meanwhile, I was free to roam the streets of the city while waiting for transportation to Albacete. I wandered around the Plaza del Sol and bought a *mono,* a coverall that I was glad to exchange for my filthy worn-out uniform. In the barracks, I bathed for the first time in weeks using a bucket of cold water and a borrowed piece of soap. I kept my helmet, which gave me a sense of security during what turned out to be two long nights of air raids.

The scars of war were evident in the besieged capital. The Prado Museum had been bombed, and the Palace of the Duke of Alba burned to the ground. But the spirit of the people could not be broken, and the city was defended thanks to Soviet tanks and airplanes. To show their gratitude, some Madrileños hung pictures of Soviet leaders in the streets and balconies. On the morning of my third day in Madrid, an army truck appeared outside the barracks to take several of us to Albacete, an all-day drive. The trip became more and more peaceful as we drove further and further away from the bombs and into the countryside of La Mancha.

In Albacete, we went straight to the Estado Mayor and spent the night there. My civilian clothing and suitcase were returned to me the following day. I reported to the American base commissar, Bill Lawrence. He and his assistant, Johnny Murra, had offices in a modern-looking building called *Círculo Mercantil.* Lawrence had been expecting me and immediately gave me an assignment. I was to set up a circulating library for the American volunteers in the rear guard, both those in training and those convalescing. Lawrence deemed the library an important task that I was to accomplish in a large room one flight down. I shared the room with an English comrade named Sydney, who had been wounded and had only partial use of his left arm. He was an artist now designing war posters. The room also served as our sleeping quarters and became my home for the next three months.

My work in the library gave me time for reflection. I was in no condition to return to the battlefield, and I had to deal with feelings of guilt about leaving my comrades to do the fighting while I was alive and sheltered here away from the horrors of battle. I counted myself damn lucky to have escaped the holocaust of Brunete all in one piece. I thought about my friend John Bowman who had traveled here with me only to be killed on the first day of battle. I thought, "Why him and not me?" And then there were all the others who fell along the way. I began to feel that fate must have spared me to carry on the good fight in other ways. After completing my library assignment, I was next assigned to work in the International Brigade Post

Office.

I was kept active and felt better about myself day by day. There were many of us working in *la retraguardia,* the rear guard. It was nothing to be ashamed of that we weren't on the front lines. The building where I worked had a crew of cleaning women, and we usually had breakfast together in a little restaurant on the ground floor. We would sit together at one long table, eating, drinking, laughing, and rubbing knees flirtatiously, though that's as far as it went. Whenever I began to show more than casual interest in one of these women, I would hear someone at the table shout "*Disciplina, camarada!*" and everyone else would burst out laughing. I loved the spirit of these brave women and how they often sang while they worked in the building. I later wondered how many of them managed to survive the Fascist tyranny after Franco seized control of the country in March of 1939.

Each day in Albacete there was the traditional afternoon *siesta*, when music and news reports came blaring from the loudspeakers in the plaza. The program would always begin with the national anthem of the Republic, "*El Hymno Riego.*" By late afternoon, the restaurant on the ground floor of the *Círculo Mercantil* was filled with Internationals, who were passing through or waiting for reassignment. Sometimes, with the help of *vino tinto,* the atmosphere became raucous. Everyone had a story to tell, and this was the best place in town to hear the latest rumors and news from all fronts in all languages.

For the most part, we were unaware of conflicts inside the Popular Front government between the various Socialist, Communist and Anarchist factions. The one thing that mattered to us volunteers was winning the war. Two months before the battle of Brunete, there had been street battles in

Barcelona, an uprising instigated by the Anarchists and a Trotskyite organization called the Workers' Party of Marxist Unity (P.O.UM.) Suspected of being agents of Franco, the P.O.U.M was subsequently outlawed when a new government was formed under Socialist Party leader Dr. Juan Negrin. Negrin replaced fellow Socialist Largo Caballero and maintained the Party's uneasy alliance with the Communists. Breaks in Popular Front unity and infighting among the various factions weakened popular resistance and surely affected the military conduct of the war. But the final outcome was primarily the result of the non-intervention policies that left the Republican army out-gunned by the Fascists.

While in Albacete, I studied Spanish with a tutor who visited the *Círculo Mercantil* most afternoons. I made such progress that I was able to meet and make a date for a movie with a young Spanish woman. She later invited me to dinner with her family. They were peasants who lived outside the city. I remember that we sat outdoors around a table, eating olives and drinking wine from a *porron*, and then ate our meal from a common platter in the center of the table. They treated me like a guest of honor, and I felt honored just to be in their presence. At that moment the war seemed far away.

One afternoon I visited the railroad station to see if I might run into anyone I knew on a troop train arriving that day. The passengers were Polish volunteers and I was about to give up when I heard someone yell, "Hey, Whitey!" Standing there in a Polish officer's uniform with a big grin on his face was Jim Harris, an old friend from the rank-and-file movement in New York. I had heard that he had been in the Lincoln Battalion at Jarama and had mysteriously disappeared. I thought he was dead, but here he was larger than life, now an officer in the Dombrowski Battalion. We stood on the platform talking excitedly until his train was ready to pull out. Jim hopped aboard, and we waved our goodbyes. That was the last I saw of Jim Harris. His name is on the honor roll of those killed in Spain.

At the end of September, while I was still working in the Brigade post office, I came down with an infection in my right foot. A doctor from New York, Bill Pike, happened to see me limping. After examining me, he quickly had me hospitalized. It was blood poisoning that had already spread to a lymph gland in my thigh. The gland had to be lanced and drained immediately, and it was pure luck that Dr. Pike had been there to treat me. I spent the next two weeks in the hospital, taking foot baths in potassium permanganate. I shared a small ward with several wounded guys who were looking forward to a well-earned rest at one of the convalescent hospitals on the Mediterranean coast.

I left the hospital in the middle of October. Having had time to think, I was beginning to seriously doubt my usefulness to the cause in Spain. I entertained fantasies about returning to sea, sometimes imagining myself in clean dungarees, standing lookout on the bow or taking my trick at the wheel. When I returned to *Círculo Mercantil,* I found the place demoralizing and became more discontent. Finally, I went back to see Bill Lawrence and asked him to send me home. I told Bill that I thought I could do more for the anti-Fascist cause by returning to my work in the maritime industry. He agreed and promised to set the wheels in motion for my repatriation. One problem that confronted me was that my passport had been confiscated while I was a prisoner in Toulouse. I would have to return to France illegally until arrangements could be made for its return.

In order to travel I needed civilian clothing and had a tailor make me a *traje* (suit) of English worsted wool. The only shoes available were the *alpargatas* that by now I was accustomed to wearing. One day at the end of the month, wearing my new suit and carrying a *salvoconducto* in my pocket, I boarded a train for Barcelona. Arriving that evening, I was met by Bill Sussman, another comrade from the rank-and-file movement in New York. He had been in charge of the committee in Paris that was responsible for getting volunteers into Spain. Bill was now the liaison in Barcelona between the French committee and the Brigade. He arranged for me to stay overnight, and the next day I left for *la frontera* (the Spanish-French border).

At the frontier I was met by *carabiñeros* (border guards), one of whom escorted me along a mountain trail. At one point he stopped and pointed toward the bottom of the trail at the foot of the mountain. He explained that I would be met there by a French comrade. I felt deep regret about leaving behind my comrades to carry on the fight, knowing many of them would never return home. The guard said *"Salud, camarada!"* and we exchanged the clenched-fist salute of the Frente Popular. With some misgivings, I headed down the trail alone, at times hopping and skipping like a mountain goat, not knowing what to expect with my prison experience in Toulouse still fresh in mind.

But this time there were no gendarmes waiting to arrest me. At the bottom of the trail, a young Frenchman greeted me with the familiar *"Salud, camarade!"* and raised his fist in the air. He spoke no English, and I spoke little French, but there was an understanding between us. We walked together into the village of Cerbére, and he took me to the office of the French Committee to Aid the Spanish People. They were expecting me. I was taken to a small restaurant for dinner and given a train ticket to Paris.

After traveling through the night, we pulled into the Gare St. Lazarre. My suit was wrinkled and I was in need of a shave. I stepped onto the station platform, wearing my beret and *alpargatas* and carrying a few francs that had been given to me by the underground in Cerbére for pocket money. The weather was sunny and mild for November. Outside the station, the street was crowded with rush hour traffic and business as usual. I called the committee and was given directions to take a Metro line to a certain station. I made good connections and soon arrived at the headquarters on the Boulevard de la Villette.

Supported by the committee, I waited in Paris while those acting on my behalf negotiated with the American authorities for the return of my passport. My room at the Hotel Louis Blanc was covered, and I had a few francs to spend on such necessities as Metro rides and showers at a public bathhouse. Near the hotel was a small restaurant where it was arranged for me to have my meals.

As soon as I settled in, I called Odette. I had written to her from Albacete and received a letter in reply and a photo of her taken on the seacoast of Brittany, where she had vacationed. We met often during the next few weeks, sometimes with her mother and sister and sometimes with her friends. Odette took afternoons off from work to go with me to the movies. We spent many hours together at the 1937 World's Fair. The Soviet and German pavilions faced each other on opposite sides of a promenade. Their global confrontation was epitomized by the statue of a Soviet man and woman holding aloft a hammer and sickle on one side, while across the way was a huge Nazi swastika.

After the committee was notified that I could retrieve my passport, I went to the American Consulate. A consular official opened a desk drawer and took out a bundle of passports, the ones that had been confiscated from us in Toulouse. He pulled mine out and stamped it "Only good for return to the U.S." There was nothing I could say or do. I was glad that I was no longer a man without a country, but had mixed feelings about leaving France. Saying goodbye to Odette was difficult, but I knew I had to return home.

At the end of November, I walked aboard the French liner *SS Lafayette* in Le Havre. My ticket to New York had been paid for by the committee. I shared a stateroom with two fellow volunteers, Carl Bradley and Bill Wheeler, who were also being repatriated from the Brigade. The trans-Atlantic passage took a week. On the voyage, I met a female passenger who was secretary to U.S. Congressman Dickstein of New York. This kind woman would lend me a helping hand some months later when I visited Washington, D.C. as a representative of the National Maritime Union.

Arriving in New York in December, we tied up at the French Line pier on Manhattan's West Side. We were met onboard by a well-dressed young man wearing a trench coat. He introduced himself as a representative of the U.S. State Department and politely asked me to surrender my passport. This was the first step in my being officially classified as a "premature anti-Fascist." I would have to wait twenty-three years before I could be issued another tourist passport.

The three of us who traveled together -- Carl, Bill, and I -- were also met by representatives of the Friends of the Lincoln Brigade. They accompanied us ashore and escorted us to the office of the Friends committee, who provided the assistance we needed to get back on our feet. I checked into the old Broadway Central Hotel for a few days, until arrangements were made for me to stay with the family of Eugene Wolman in Mount Vernon. Eugene had been with me in the Washington Battalion and was killed in the Brunete offensive. His mother and father deeply appreciated hearing about their son from someone who had been with him in Spain and witnessed his bravery.

Mr. Wolman drove me into New York City on his way to work, and I headed straight for the National Maritime Union office on West 17th Street. I was given an honorary membership in the NMU in recognition for my work on the strike committee during 1936 Spring Strike and my status as a veteran of the Lincoln Brigade. In those days most CIO unions were democratic and under progressive leadership. There were always plenty of ships tied up at the docks in Manhattan and Brooklyn, and the NMU controlled most of the hiring.

Eager to ship out, I checked in at the union hiring hall each day to see what jobs were available. On the day after Christmas, I presented my three-week-old shipping card to the dispatcher for an AB job on a Moore-McCormack Scantic Line freighter going to the Baltic. There were guys around with older cards than mine, but they must have wanted to stay ashore for the holidays. The next day I signed on the *SS Scanmail* as an AB for $72.50 per month, and we sailed that same afternoon for Copenhagen.

The Atlantic crossing took a couple of weeks, which gave the crew time to get acquainted and hold our first union meeting. We elected a ship's committee composed of delegates from the deck, engine, and stewards departments. I was elected as deck delegate. The crew was a congenial bunch—except for the bo's'n, who was a company man. Back at sea again after fourteen months, I was doing all the things sailors do and feeling great about it. And yet there wasn't a day that went by that my thoughts and dreams didn't return to Spain. The sights and sounds and smells still haunted me: the fierce crackle of gunfire, the smell of the trenches, the booming roar and glare of bombs, the mountain dawns over pine forests and glittering ancient villages, the stamp of boots in the barracks, the faces of the people that carried their anguish with such dignity.

We discharged our cargo in Copenhagen, then followed an ice-breaker into the Gulf of Finland. I wandered aimlessly around the cold streets of Helsinki in the winter darkness, feeling like the stranger I was. After stops in Gydinia, Stockholm and Gaevle, we made a stormy twelve-day back across the North Atlantic. Shortly after my return to New York, I went to a union meeting at which we discussed upcoming congressional hearings on the subject of safety at sea. After a motion was made and passed unanimously to send a rank-and-file delegation to testify before Congress, the floor was opened for nominations. My name was one of those put before the membership for a vote. R. Francis Kennedy, Patrick Codyre and I were elected to represent the National Maritime Union at hearings conducted by the House Committee on Education and Labor.

We arrived in Washington D.C. the next day and went directly to Capitol Hill. Heads turned as we walked into the hearing room. We were dressed in dungarees, pea coats and watch caps. I heard a few dismissive chuckles as the names Kennedy, Codyre, and Cullinen were announced and put in the official record. We were each given a few minutes to speak our piece, each of us making the case for our union's role in protecting of the welfare of merchant seamen. In my mind defending the rights of workers here on the home front was the same cause that had taken me to Spain.

When the hearing was over, my two colleagues headed back to New York, and I stayed on to attend the last day of a conference of the American Youth Congress. Some YCL comrades of mine who were at the conference decided to organize a picket line in front of the German Embassy on the following day. They wanted to protest the Nazi presence in Washington and also to test a new law that made it illegal to picket within five hundred feet of any foreign embassy. I went along knowing that we were risking arrest.

Within minutes after we had gathered in front of the embassy and started shouting anti-Fascist slogans, the police rounded us up and hauled us off to jail. After an unpleasant night in the hoosegow, we were released on bail and forbidden to leave the city while awaiting trial. This was my first time in the nation's capital, but it didn't take me long to find my way around thanks to a network of fraternal organizations and my friend Rhoda, who introduced me to her college friends at George Washington University. Congressman Dickstein's secretary offered her support by allowing me to stay in her apartment.

A month later we went to trial in Federal District Court and received suspended sentences. Judge Curran looked me straight in the eye and said, "Cullinen! I want you to go back to New York and ship out!" Those may have been some of the kindest words ever spoken to me, and I was more than happy to comply with his instructions.

Back in New York in April, I threw in my shipping card for an job on the *SS Talamanca* of the "Great White Fleet, plenty of work and nothing to eat." The food was better than before the '37 strike, though there was still room for improvement. It was obvious to me, after sailing on so many United Fruit Company ships over the years, that conditions had improved for the unlicensed crew. But the officers aboard were still behind the times. One in particular, Mr. McCoy, the third mate, was the epitome of a company man. We always rubbed each other the wrong way, especially after I was elected as chairman of the ship's committee. After that, we regarded each other as natural enemies whenever we sailed together.

Over the next three and a half months. I made four trips on the *Talamanca,* two as AB and two as quartermaster. We were on a regular run from New York to the Caribbean and Latin America, spending time in Kingston, Jamaica; Cartagena, Colombia; and Puerto Limón, Costa Rica. Going ashore in these ports was always a splendid time for passengers and crew. I had my share of fun and liked my job despite McCoy. The *Talamanca* was a terrific ship, and I would have stayed on her longer if it weren't for a chance misfortune.

While alongside the dock in New York during August, I had an accident that terminated my job. As I was walking through the hold, I hit the top of my head on the edge of the steel frame of a watertight door. Fortunately, I was with an NMU patrolman named Rodriguez who had come aboard to collect union dues. I saw a few stars and blacked out, falling to the deck. The next thing I knew Rodriguez was helping me up and blood was streaming down my face. He took me to the company medical office on the dock. A doctor shaved the top of my head and closed the wound in my scalp with steel clamps.

I spent the next three months on the beach in New York, collecting workmen's compensation. At this time I fell in with a group of talented people lived in a walk-up loft on West Twenty-Eighth Street. The occupants of the building were anti-Fascists and very willing to help a veteran of the Lincoln Brigade. On the first floor was a modern dancer, Mura Dehn, who had a large dance studio behind her living space. A well-known photographer, Gus Bundy had his living quarters and dark room on the second floor. Gus turned me on to photography and taught me the black-and-white process from beginning to end. On Sunday mornings, we sometimes strolled through the Lower East Side with our cameras, later returning to the darkroom to develop and print the pictures. I lived on the third floor of the building in one corner of a large studio occupied by Michael Loew, an artist later known for his murals at the 1939 World's Fair in Flushing Meadows.

By October 1938, I had been on the beach in New York for more than two months. I heard a story circulating on the waterfront that a ship was being chartered by the North American Committee to Aid Spanish Democracy. It was the *SS Erica Reed,* an old Hog Island freighter. She had hired a crew in New Orleans and was now headed for New York to load a cargo of food, clothing, and medical supplies for the beleaguered Spanish Republic. There were rumors that some members of the crew had vowed to create an international incident by organizing a sit-down strike in Barcelona to attempt to discredit the Popular Front. It turned out that these characters were an insignificant minority among the NMU crew. They were so unpopular with their shipmates that they were forced to abandon ship in New York, thereby creating a few jobs.

Of course, I had a special interest in this ship. I wanted to join her crew because I felt a strong allegiance to my comrades still fighting in Spain. Shipping out would be an opportunity for me to help the cause in another way. I was in the hiring hall when the dispatcher posted the job for the *Erica Reed*. Having the oldest card in the hall, I was hired. It was that simple. No more fink halls or crimp joints; no more waiting in the cold outside the company shipping master's office.

I signed on as an AB on November 1, 1938. From the first day, I could see that most of the crew understood the importance of the voyage. They identified with their Spanish trade union counterparts in the struggle against Fascism. The trans-Atlantic crossing was slow in those days. At an average speed of twelve knots, it took almost two weeks to reach the Straits of Gibraltar. The crossing gave us time to get to know each other as we settled down to our normal sea watches of four hours on, eight hours off.

The ship was under the command of Captain Johnson, a loyal union man from the West Coast. Next in line was Chief Mate David Gomez, a "Gallego," originally from Spain and a staunch anti-Fascist. Then there was Reed, the Second Mate, and Cooke, the Third Mate—all of them union men. Joe Menduiña, another anti-Fascist "Gallego," was the best bo's'n I ever sailed with. There were outstanding men in all three departments, but one guy in the "Black Gang" who stood out was Gary Garabedian, a militant rank-and-filer who on more than one occasion struck fear into the hearts of the shipowners' stooges on the waterfront.

Around the middle of November, we entered the Straits of Gibraltar. As we passed into the Mediterranean, a small naval vessel flying the red and yellow flag of the Spanish Fascists steamed alongside, displaying an international code flag signal. They were asking about our destination and the nature of our cargo. Captain Johnson decided to ignore them, continuing to hold course and speed, as we were in international waters. Nothing happened for a few minutes as we steamed along, side by side, no more than four hundred feet apart. Everyone came out on deck to watch. I had just taken the wheel and heard the discussion between the chief mate and the skipper. I could see the signal flag on the Fascist gunboat was being lowered and replaced with a new one. It was an order for us to stop our ship immediately.

Their gun crews, fore and aft, trained guns on us, an unarmed merchant vessel flying the American flag. There were tense moments while we waited for our captain's decision. He finally gave orders loud and clear to hold course and speed, muttering, "To hell with these sons-of-bitches." We breathed a collective sigh of relief when the Fascist pirates veered off and disappeared in the direction of Spanish Morocco.

A few days later we tied up in Barcelona and were greeted by some familiar faces on the dock. One of them was my New Orleans friend, Red Mouton. Like the rest of the Abraham Lincoln Brigade still in Spain, Red was waiting to be repatriated. A decision had been made by the Popular Front to send home the remaining International Brigades as a last desperate effort to get the U.S. to lift the arms embargo.

I invited Red aboard one day to meet the gang and join us for lunch. We had just begun eating when the air raid sirens started wailing. Outside, the sky lit up with anti-aircraft tracers. These raids went on day and night for the entire week that we were in port, and during each raid, the longshoremen and the ship's crew were supposed to run down the gangway and along the dock to the *refugio* (air raid shelter) to await the all-clear signals. On the day that Red visited, the drill was carried out as usual with one exception. Red remained at the table in the mess room, his appetite overcoming his fear.

At the end of the week, we said our goodbyes and steamed slowly out of the harbor, picking our way carefully between the masts of sunken ships. None of us imagined at that point that Barcelona would fall to the Fascists within months. We were headed for a British naval base at Malta to load up with bunkers, fresh water, and stores. We spent the night there, enjoying beer, whiskey, rum, and some pretty Maltese girls. Our orders came the following morning from Spain. We were to proceed to Istanbul and await further instructions. After another day crossing the Mediterranean, we pulled into the busy harbor of Istanbul, dropped the hook and went ashore. Again it was beer, whiskey, ouzo, baklava, and the red light district.

After two days at anchor, we received orders to sail to Odessa and wait for further orders. I assumed that we would be loading another cargo in Odessa for return to Barcelona or Valencia, since the only countries supplying Loyalist forces were the Soviet Union and Mexico. We headed out from Istanbul through the narrow Straits of Bosporus and into the Black Sea. As we passed through the Straits, we were close to shore, so close that we could hear barking dogs, human voices, and oriental music; we even got an occasional whiff of Turkish coffee. But there was no time for daydreaming of baklava and belly dancers. We were looking forward to a week in Soviet Russia, then a quick return to Spain. Little did we know what lay in store for us.

We arrived at the dock in Odessa on a gray, cold day in December. As soon as we had tied up and lowered the gangway, a delegation of Soviet officials in long, heavy overcoats and fur hats appeared on the dock. One of them yelled up to Captain Johnson, who was on the wing of the bridge, “Captain! Vy are you in Odessa?” Then they came aboard and went up to the bridge. After about a half hour, they all came out of the captain’s room and went back ashore. The word soon spread that we would be welcome to take on fresh water and stores, but we would have to leave the dock the next day and go out to anchor in the harbor. The Russians had no information about our ship, and since we had not paid a port entry fee, we would have to lay in port while waiting for orders. Under the circumstances, there was no shore leave.

Frustrated and disappointed, we laid at anchor in Odessa for fifty-two days during the bleak months of December and January. There was nothing to relieve the boredom except work. We chipped rust, red-leaded and painted from stem to stern. On the watch below, there was little to do but read and discuss the latest radio news reports. The Popular Front had not yet fallen, but the military situation had been steadily deteriorating since the spring when Franco's forces reached the Mediterranean and broke the Republican territory in two.

At the end of January, our orders from Spain came through in the form of a radiogram. We were to proceed immediately to Marseilles to load a cargo of flour, which was being trans-shipped by rail from Antwerp. The flour destined for Spain had been waiting inexplicably on the dock in Antwerp since December. We later learned from our radio operator that we had been the victims of sabotage by Fascist infiltrators who sent us on a wild goose chase. We arrived in Marseilles in mid-February and began loading our cargo. It took a week or so, during which time we enjoyed the pleasures of this French seaport. For us sailors, this visit to port was like being released from prison after our two-month confinement.

After leaving with our cargo, we sailed for Cartagena. Before entering the harbor, we were met by a Loyalist torpedo boat. The officer in charge cautioned us to avoid Cartagena and head north to Alicante. He said there had been a Fascist attempt to seize control of Cartagena and that city wasn't safe. We reached Alicante the next day. As soon as we tied up, longshoremen came aboard and went to work on the long overdue cargo. We were elated that we had overcome so many obstacles and finally delivered the goods. But that feeling was not to last long.

Shortly after unloading the flour onto the dock, we heard the familiar wail of air raid sirens. We left the ship and crowded into a shelter at the head of the dock and waited for bombs to drop. Soon we heard muffled explosions and anti-aircraft fire. We huddled together, cursing the Nazi Heinkels and Mussolini's Caproni bombers. There were angry, blasphemous outbursts from the longshoremen -- *"Me cago en Dios," "Me cago en la ostia," "Me cago en la virgin,"* and referring to the Italian bombers, *"Me cago en los trimotores."* A half hour later we heard the welcome sound of the all-clear signal.

Coming out of the shelter, we were dumbfounded to see our ship halfway out in the channel with only one head line holding her to the dock. There was a launch waiting to take us to a Jacob's ladder on the offshore side. Once we were back on board, we headed to sea again. We were told that during the air raid, the captain and radio operator had stayed aboard and received new orders. We were to leave Alicante and sail to Valencia, which was now the capital of the Republic. Traitors had control of the army in Madrid and were in the process of capitulating to Franco. Negrin and his cabinet had been forced to move the government to Valencia. This was a final desperate effort to hold out against the combined forces of the Fascist powers and allow time for political, military and union leaders of the Popular Front to get out of the country. Those who remained went into the underground if they were not captured and murdered by the Fascists.

We were in Valencia more than a week. One night at the headquarters of the Socorro Rojo Internacíonal, I joined a group of volunteers who were going into the streets with paintbrushes and buckets of whitewash. Sensing the end was near, we painted the word *"RESISTIR"* on walls and buildings all over the city. It was to be the last defiant slogan of the dying Spanish Republic.

We finished discharging our cargo of flour and sailed out of Valencia on March 9, 1939 with twelve stowaways on board. Everyone, including the captain, knew of their presence. We were saving them from certain death at the hands of Franco. One of the stowaways, Ettore Fontana was an Italian-American from Connecticut and a member of the Lincoln Brigade. Ettore had been stranded in Valencia after being hospitalized and losing his passport. The whole gang went ashore with him in Marseilles. We drank beer at the Elephant and Castle Bar and said our goodbyes to Ettore. There is no record that he ever returned to the States. If he stayed in France, he may have joined the anti-Fascist underground during World War II, which was only another six months away.

We waited at the dock in Marseilles for three weeks hoping to receive further orders, but none were forthcoming. We were simply thanked for completing our mission. Although expected, the news was stunning and tragic: the war had come to an end with Franco's criminal regime installed in Madrid. The anti-Fascist cause may have been defeated in Spain, but I was determined to carry its ideals home with me. They were clasped in my heart when I arrived back in New York in mid-April, grateful to be alive and fully aware that the 'good fight' was far from over.

Chapter Four

The War against Fascism Continues / 1939 - 1946

Back in New York in the springtime with a five-and-a-half-month payoff in my pocket, I sensed for the first time in my life what it must be like to be rich. At the rate of $72.50 per month minus a few small draws in port, I paid off the *Erica Reed* with about $325. After putting down a five-dollar deposit on a furnished room, I established a savings account, something I hadn't done since I was a kid in Red Bluff.

Wanting to try my luck ashore, I took a job in a cosmetics factory within walking distance from where I was living on West 23rd Street. I learned more about making lipstick than I ever wanted to know. The process entailed heating chemical ingredients until they became liquid, then pouring the raw material into molds. The finished product was put it into dispensers labeled with fancy French names. The factory was a small operation that employed about fifteen workers. My boss wore a white coat and called himself a chemist. He kept to himself and was usually lurking in the background. The rest of the gang was friendly, but I sensed that I would eventually have trouble with him.

After two weeks, I was invited to a birthday party in Forest Hills for one of the young female workers. In those days before television, people would gather around the piano and sing songs or do comedy acts. That night we took turns performing for the amusement of the rest of the group. When my turn came, I sang a Spanish revolutionary song, "*La Joven Guardia,*" uncertain how my choice would be accepted. To my surprise, the song was well received and stimulated a lively discussion about the defeat of the Spanish Republic and the growing threat of Fascism.

A short time later I arranged a lunch meeting with a union organizer at a restaurant in the neighborhood. I brought a half dozen of my co-workers and after listening to the organizer, we decided to invite the union to try to organize the factory. The next morning, I was summoned to appear before the man in the white coat. He coolly handed me my paycheck and said my services were no longer required. No reason was given, but it was obvious that someone fingered me as a troublemaker. Without a union contract, I had no one to defend me.

Unemployed again, I decided to go back to sea. My NMU shipping card had matured to the point where I could almost have my pick of jobs. In June of 1939, I signed on as an AB on the S*S Oriente.* The ship made a regular run between New York and Havana, carrying passengers, mail and some cargo. The round trip took a week, with a day and a night on each end. We sailed from New York on Sundays and arrived in Havana every Tuesday morning, making about thirty rounds trips over the next four and a half months.

Depending on one's point of view, Havana at the time was either a hedonistic paradise or a cesspool of debauchery. It was said that if you put a roof over the whole city, it would be like one big whorehouse. The gambling casinos were a major source of profit for the American mob, and the city was the pleasure capital of the Caribbean until the 1959 revolution, led by Fidel Castro, Che Guevara and Camilo Cienfuegos, abolished the old order of corruption and exploitation.

For a sailor with American dollars to spend on shore leave in 1939 Havana, the dazzling night life offered endless temptations. There were times when I succumbed, but I had other pressing interests. I was following the events in Europe closely and making new political contacts. I soon met Arnaldo Odio, a dentist who had studied in Washington, D.C, and his brother-in-law, Armando Hart, who was later appointed Minister of Education by Castro. Among the crew of the *Oriente,* I helped organize an NMU committee and attended a meeting of the Cuban Longshoremen's Union as part of a delegation from our ship. We offered fraternal greetings from the NMU and promised our support in the event of a strike. Politics was much on my mind. We radicals had foreseen the Fascist peril in Spain, and after the fall of the Republic, Hitler attacked Poland and opened World War II, proving the folly of non-intervention and appeasement policies.

I was finally paid off in New York in early November and moved in with one of my shipmates, Bob Wilt, who lived in the Lower East Side. Bob invited me to stay as long as I wished. He and his family were politically progressive and felt their hospitality was the least they could do for a veteran of the Lincoln Brigade. During the Christmas holidays, a surprise guest arrived. Another Lincoln veteran, Al Hawkey, had driven to New York from Mexico City in his seven-passenger Packard limousine. The car was a sight to behold, with a plate glass window separating the rear passenger compartment from the front seat, and a speaking tube for the chauffeur.

Al was taking passengers back and forth between Mexico City and New York for fifty dollars a head. The round trip took about two weeks and netted him about a thousand a month if all six seats were filled both ways. Gas was cheap, but recruiting passengers was difficult at times. Al suggested I share the driving and accompany him to Mexico for a reduced fare of $20. Off I went with my 35mm camera, a record player, and my record collection including Tino Rossi singing "*J'attendrai toujours*."

We arrived in Mexico City early in January under a clear blue sky, as the city had not yet been fouled by pollution. Even in the heart of the city, the air was rich with the scent of flowers and tropical fruits being sold at sidewalk stands. In the distance was the magnificent sight of snow-covered Ixi (Ixtaxihuatl) and Popo (Popocatepetl), both extinct volcanoes that were once sacred to the Aztecs. I was thrilled as we pulled up to the curb along the Paseo de la Reforma and delivered our passengers.

Al invited me to stay temporarily at an apartment he shared with an American newspaper correspondent, Joan Wemple. Her place was within walking distance of the Palacio de Bellas Artes. Among her visitors was a young American artist named Stanley Koppel, who soon invited me to stay at his rooftop pad while he was away on a sketching trip. I moved in and had the place to myself temporarily. This was the perfect arrangement given my limited budget. I had already spent most of my payoff from the *SS Oriente,* but I was able to get by with the help of a growing network of new friends, some of whom like me had fought in Spain.

After the defeat of the Popular Front in the spring of 1939, a number of anti-Fascist refugees, including veterans of the International Brigades, found a haven in Mexico. Most were unsung heroes trying to build new lives for themselves, while a few were well known among political circles. One of these who I came to know was David Alfaro Siqueiros, a famous Mexican artist who was also a leader of the Communist Party. On one occasion he invited me to watch him paint a series of murals on a new building that housed the Electrical Workers Union on the Reforma. Siqueiros believed that public murals were a powerful medium for communicating his vision of class struggle to a broad audience. He had been jailed and expelled from Mexico a number of times for his political activities. The year after I met him, he was forced into exile in America for fictitious allegations that he had played a role in the assassination of Leon Trotsky.

Another International Brigades veteran who befriended me was Ludwig Renn. A former career officer in the German army, Renn had trained officers for the Loyalist army in Spain, and after the war he had been interned there. Earlier in his life, he had been an anti-Nazi author and was imprisoned in Germany for several years for “literary high treason.” When I met him he was a history professor at the University of Morelia and served as president of the Latin American Committee for Free Germans. He lived in a beautiful *hacienda* -- he called it La Torre Blanca -- in Tacuba, a suburb of Mexico City. There were at least ten rooms in his home, and several were always occupied by visiting artists and writers from *el norte.*

Everyone in my new circle of friends found their way to La Torre Blanca. One guest, a woman writer from the States, invited me to spend the night with her there. The next morning while we were having breakfast on the patio with some of the other guests, Ludwig walked out in his birthday suit for his morning sunbath. I may have been the only one surprised at his naked appearance. As he stretched out in the sun, the other guests were sophisticated enough to exchange casual greetings with Ludwig. I thought the way he exhibited himself was carried off with a marvelous lack of phony pretense. At that moment I was reminded again how far I had come from my early Catholic upbringing.

In March, Stan Koppel returned from his sketching trip and decided to head back to California. Fortunately, Dr. Cesar Rosenbaum arrived from New York at the about the same time and rented a place across the street. Cesar generously invited me to share the space. He wasn't practicing medicine, but he did occasionally write out free prescriptions for those in need. He once treated me for Montezuma's Revenge and was one of those who helped me survive three months south of the border. I never missed a meal and even though I had to sell my phonograph and record collection to bring in money, I lived modestly well.

I was surprised one day when another old comrade-in-arms, Larry O'Toole, blew into town. Larry was en route from New York to San Francisco, but like many of us veterans, he was drawn south of the border because Mexico had been the only country in the Western hemisphere that had openly supported the Spanish Republic. I was somewhat intrigued when Larry told me in passing about a young woman named Florence whom he had met recently in New York and whose husband had been killed in Spain. Larry stayed with me only a few days, then continued his trip to California.

I was getting near the end of my rope and longing to be back at sea. After trying unsuccessfully to find a job on a ship in Vera Cruz, I decided as a stranded American citizen to appeal to U.S. Ambassador Joseph Daniels for help. This venerable gentleman was an FDR appointee, and he was kind enough to listen to my story. But he offered no assistance except to suggest that I find a ride with someone returning to the States. I had no choice but to take his advice and soon managed to find a good Samaritan with a brand new red Pontiac convertible who was about to drive north.

The fellow agreed to take me as far as Chicago in return for my sharing the driving. The only problem was that he decided to stop for several days of hunting halfway to the border in a town called Ciudad Victoria. There he checked into a hotel, paid for a double room, and asked me to wait until he returned from his hunting trip. The hotel was adequate except for the occasional hairy-legged tarantula that dropped from the chandelier and scurried across the floor. By the second day, I was growing anxious about the arrangement and my finances. The room was paid for, but I still had to eat and was running out of money.

As I stood in front of the hotel feeling some desperation, a Mexican teenager passed by and we struck up a conversation. The boy was surprised that I spoke the language. He was curious about me, sensing that I wasn't a typical gringo tourist. I asked him to recommend an inexpensive restaurant, and he exclaimed, "*Hombre, sí usted tiene hambre, venga conmigo a mi casa. Tenemos bastante para comer.*" I trusted him intuitively, accepted his invitation and followed. We walked together to his home in a slum area populated by stray cats, mongrel dogs, pigs, chickens, and raggedy barefoot children. He led me into a one-room adobe hut and introduced me to his teenage wife and their two small children.

They lived without plumbing or electricity and had only a charcoal fire for cooking. The boy and I sat at a small table in the semi-darkness while his wife prepared tortillas and beans. She soon brought the meal to the table and joined us. As we sat there eating, talking and laughing, I couldn't help thinking that we had so much in common under the skin as members of the human family. I was inspired by these impoverished Mexicans who were so willing to share what little they had with a *gringo.* As a result of similar experiences I had by now all over the world, like my sharing food with Spanish peasants and Filipino jungle dwellers, I was coming to appreciate more and more that we are deeply bonded as a species, that we have too much in common to remain forever divided.

Later in life when I became aware of Ashley Montagu's work, he struck me as on the mark when he said that the only reason we have survived as a species is that the constructive forces in human nature outweigh the destructive forces. I took him to mean that we humans have a phenomenal ability in times of crisis to band together and cooperate for the common good despite the rattlesnakes in our midst, modern rattlers ranging from profiteering multinational corporations to drug cartels and what later became known as the "military-industrial complex."

The fellow with the red Pontiac showed up again as promised, and we finished our journey. I was left outside Chicago and hitched back to New York. Once again in April of 1940, I found myself homeless, broke and increasingly desperate in a city of strangers, feeling like the abandoned child I once was. I soon turned to old friends and the office of the Veterans of the Lincoln Brigade. They provided money for a hotel room and food until I could find a job. I went to the NMU hall on 17th Street to get a shipping card. There were plenty of jobs posted every day, and after about a month my card was old enough to be competitive.

During that month, I met a woman named Florence at the old Manhattan Center Ballroom on Thirty-Fourth Street. The occasion was the Annual Ball of the National Maritime Union. This was the era of the Lindy, and the Jitterbugs danced circles around me to Benny Goodman, Glen Miller,

Artie Shaw, and Tommy Dorsey. With a few beers under my belt, I had the courage to ask one of the prettiest girls in the place for a dance, and she turned out to be none other than Larry O'Toole's girlfriend, Florence. We began a romance but both of us harbored guilt for betraying Larry, who was only temporarily out of the picture. The triangle played itself out soon enough. He came back to town and hooked up again with Florence, who eventually married him. I went back to sea.

On May 11, 1940, I signed on the *SS City of Baltimore* as AB for $72.50 a month. She was a combination passenger ship and freighter bound for the Caribbean and the Panama Canal. I saw a marked improvement in working and living conditions on board, with two men to a room instead of the old crowded fo'c'sle. The food wasn't bad either, and we were now paid time-and-a-half for overtime.

Early on a Saturday morning, I was sound asleep in my bunk after a night of making the rounds of the cabarets in Colon with my shipmates. As in a dream, I heard a familiar voice saying, "Rise and shine for the Panama Pacific Line. Wake up, George, it's chow time!" I opened my eyes and looked up into the grinning face of Joe Young. The last time I had seen him was in Albacete in August of 1937. I later heard that Joe had been captured and hadn't known if he had come through alive. Our unexpected reunion came about as he had arrived in the Canal zone the day before working on another American ship. Somehow he found out that I was here, and we spent the day ashore bringing each other up to date.

Joe had been captured by the Fascists during the retreat on the Ebro front in the spring of 1938. Up until that time, Franco's forces had taken few prisoners, usually torturing them and leaving them to die on the battlefield. Joe attributed his good luck to the fact that he was wearing a crucifix, which was spotted by an Italian officer in the nick of time. He and a number of other Americans were held prisoner in Burgos until September 1939. Because his name was at the end of the alphabet, he was one of the last Americans to be released.

I returned to New York and signed off the *SS City of Baltimore* on July 21, 1940, just one day before France surrendered to the Nazis. The fabled Maginot Line was no match for Hitler's panzer divisions. I later saw newsreel footage of a jubilant Hitler dancing his little jig on the Champs Elysées, and I thought of Odette and wondered how she and her friends would survive.

Shipping was slow out of the NMU hall that summer. In desperation, I threw in my card as an ordinary seaman on the *SS Panama,* one of three new sister passenger ships belonging to the Panama Railroad Line. We shipped out for the Caribbean on July 9. The fact that I was overqualified worked to my advantage, as I quickly won the confidence of my shipmates and was elected chairman of the ship's committee. During the next four and a half months at sea, we had a number of union meetings. Discussions raged about the war in Europe and what position the union should take regarding the proposed military draft. Most of us saw the threat of Fascism in class terms, with the Axis powers hellbent on crushing working class resistance everywhere they conquered as well as carrying out genocide against the Jews. In little more than a year, we had seen the Nazi occupation of Austria, Czechoslovakia, half of Poland, Belgium, and The Netherlands, as well the surrender of France and the bombing of Great Britain.

During this period a border war was being fought between Finland and the Soviet Union. The Finns, under the leadership of a self-proclaimed Fascist, Baron Von Mannerheim, were making a flank attack on Leningrad, while Mannheim's Nazi friends in Berlin were maneuvering in preparation for the eventual *blitzkrieg* against Moscow. While Stalin had tried to buy time by making his pact with Hitler in the spring of 1939, we veterans were bonded by our fierce anti-Fascism. We ultimately had no choice but to support American entry in the war. But another year would pass before the shock of Pearl Harbor would finally force the U.S. to enter the fray.

After seven round trips on the *SS Panama,* I was paid off in New York in November and found myself $7-a-week room on the West Side. I registered for a new shipping card at the NMU hall, but I was in no hurry to ship out. On a Saturday in early December, I saw an item that caught my interest in the "What's On" column of the *Daily Worker*, announcing the Annual Ball of the Artists and Writers Union. The ball took place at Webster Hall on East 11th Street. I dressed up that evening in my only go-ashore outfit, hormones working overtime. I didn't know what to expect and simply hoped for the best as always. But the best that night turned out better than I had ever dreamed.

Her name was Sonia Robbins. Artie Shaw's band played "Begin the Beguine," and I edged around the sidelines of the crowded ballroom. After exchanging greetings with a few friends, suddenly she and I came face to face. Sonia smiled and asked me if I could dance, then took me by the hand and led me onto the dance floor. We spent the rest of the evening together and made a date to meet again at the annual dinner of the Veterans of the Lincoln Brigade. That affair took place at the Hotel Diplomat in midtown. There was a dance band and a flamenco guitarist sang anti-Fascist songs like "*Sí Me Quieres Escribir*." After that night there was no separating Sonia and me.

Sonia's background was Russian-Jewish, and her original family name was Rabinowitz. Sonia was politically active on the left and was a former modern barefoot dancer of the Isadora Duncan school. Our shared political ideals in many ways provided a stable foundation for our relationship. Sonia opened up new worlds for me culturally and socially. Before we met, my knowledge theater and the arts was limited. With Sonia, I attended my first ballet, *Les Sylphides,* and found myself enchanted with the music of Chopin. I began to think about how far I had come since my days of riding freight trains and panhandling. Sonia introduced me to her friends, many of whom were artists, and to her Russian-Jewish family. She lived with her parents, younger brother and grandmother in Weehawken, New Jersey, a ferry ride across the Hudson River. Her father owned a corset factory in nearby Union City. Her brother, Jerome Robbins, was a ballet dancer destined to become an international celebrity in the field of dance and musical theater.

Although Sonia was working as a bookkeeper in the family business, her main interest since childhood had been dance. A prodigy, she had performed solo at the age of five at Carnegie Hall. Sonia later encouraged her brother to pursue dance as a career and they appeared in a number of productions together. At Camp Tamiment the year before I met him, Jerry had choreographed a short sketch called *Death of a Loyalist* about the Spanish Civil War. Like many artists and writers at the time, he supported the Communist Party during the war years.

Sonia and I temporarily shared a small apartment in West New York with her friends, Rose and Jim. Rose was Jewish, and Jim was Irish, a fact that he never let us forget. We were given a single bed in the kitchen, which was comfortable enough for a young couple in love. In the morning most of the household activity took place around the kitchen table while

Rose was making breakfast and Jim was dressing. There was no end to his anti-British jokes thanks to childhood memories of the Irish struggle for independence. We often talked politics as we saw Europe being overrun by the war machines of Hitler and Mussolini. That winter and spring of 1941 was like a brief intermission in a deadly game that seemed obvious to us, yet it would take time for most Americans to recognize how dire the situation was.

Our love nest was sweet while it lasted. The only problem was that I had to earn a living and the only work I could depend on was going back to sea. I took an AB job on a coal boat, the *SS Thomas P. Beal*, running coast-wise. The job was so unpleasant that few men stayed onboard more than a couple of trips. I was ready to leave after only one tour. The old ship was covered with coal dust from stem to stern. When Sonia drove the family car to the dock to meet me, I was covered with enough dust to be taken for a chimney sweep.

Soon thereafter, I contacted my father's cousin, Basil Anglin, who was the Industrial Relations Manager for the Texas Company. One word from him was all it took for me to land an AB job on a new Texas Company tanker, the *SS Oklahoma.* Many of the crew were company men, and there was little I could do to change their minds. In a way these guys were reaping the benefits of all of our recent organizing work in the maritime industry. In fact, they were being used by the bosses in a campaign to undermine the unions. The thought that cousin Basil was probably one of the architects of this nefarious strategy put me in an awkward position. I soon quit the job and returned to Weehawken.

Shipping had improved at New York's NMU hall, and I signed on the *SS Siboney* as deck storekeeper. She was a medium-sized passenger ship bound for Lisbon to pick up refugees from war-torn Europe. After completing that mission, I made one final trip to the Caribbean as quarter-master on the *SS Jamaica*, a United Fruit Company ship. At the end of April, I quit my job on the *Jamaica*, and Sonia and I decided to get married. The only condition on which we both agreed was that I would find a job ashore. I was soon hired as a rigger in the Bethlehem Shipyard in Hoboken and immediately joined the Shipyard Workers Union.

On May 8, 1941, a brief marriage ceremony was held in the office of Mayor Meister in Weehawken. Present at the ceremony were Sonia's mother and father, one of her aunts, Gert, and her brother who was best man. Afterwards, I was welcomed into the Rabinowitz's large extended family with a celebration began that didn't end until late the following evening. Sonia's bedroom in the family home became our bridal suite. I moved in with one battered suitcase and my sea bag, along with my sea boots and oilskins. I thought I had come home from the sea at last.

I continued working as a rigger in the Hoboken shipyard, earning eighty-five cents an hour, with time-and-a-half for overtime and double time on Sundays and holidays. That was a good income in 1941. Sonia was also earning a salary at the factory, and we were able to buy our first car that year, a secondhand Ford V-8 convertible coupe with a rumble seat. I worked through the summer and fall in the shipyard rigging loft under the watchful eye of my Scandinavian boss, old Axel. Popeye, as he was called, taught me some of the finer points of wire splicing. We spent more and more time out in the yard working aboard ships in drydock.

With the Nazi invasion of the Soviet Union in July 1941, a new phase opened in the war against Fascism. In the shipyard, we were kept busy installing three-inch guns on the fo'c'sle head and five-inch guns back aft on the poop deck of Soviet freighters. British ships were already armed. We also spliced wire spanners between the lifeboat davits, then spliced man-ropes to the spanners. I worked most weekends during 1941 installing life-saving equipment on a number of Soviet ships.

There were no female riggers employed in the yard. Since the shipyard was filled to capacity most of the time, we were sometimes transported from the yard to work on ships tied up on the Hudson River. On these occasions we carried our tools with us. One day while working on a Soviet freighter, I was approached by one of the Russian crew who asked me if *she* could borrow my marlinspike. I was surprised and delighted to see a young woman performing the duties of an able-bodied seaman, a living example of women's liberation.

One afternoon a short time later, I was assigned to replace sweat battens in the lower hold of a freighter. Working on the side of the hold ten feet above the deck, I slipped and fell back, landing in a crouched position. The impact caused my head to snap back so abruptly that I felt as if my neck were broken. I was rushed to the company infirmary, given first aid and assigned to sick leave. The whiplash kept me out of commission for nearly a month, during which I drew workman's compensation and made regular visits to the company's physical therapist.

While I convalesced, we moved with Sonia's parents to a large apartment in Weehawken on the border between West New York and New Jersey. I soon returned to my rigging job and often commuted to the shipyard by bus. Then Sonia found a cozy one-bedroom apartment in Manhattan's Chelsea district. I commuted by ferry to the shipyard in Hoboken, and Sonia took a job in a dry cleaning business owned by Sam Berkowitz, who happened to be a veteran of the Lincoln Brigade.

News from Europe was getting worse by the day. Leningrad was under siege and the Red Army was retreating, leaving a scorched earth in the path of Hitler's advancing panzer divisions. The U.S. departed from official neutrality with the lend-lease program. Many Americans believed that we might continue aiding the British and Russians and somehow avoid entering the war ourselves. That delusion was shattered by Pearl Harbor.

The afternoon of December 7, 1941 was a normal day in the shipyard, with riggers, welders, burners, pipefitters, electricians and painters going about their regular duties. Suddenly, with whistles blowing and sirens wailing, the news of the Japanese attack spread through the yard like wildfire. For the next few days rumors and questions flew and we heard reports of the damage. Within hours of the attack, Roosevelt declared war on the Axis Powers. Nazi U-boats soon began sinking American ships. Torpedoed oil tankers could be seen exploding and burning from the boardwalks along the New Jersey coast. Dead crewmen washed ashore almost daily. The war that we had fought so hard in Spain to prevent was now claiming American victims. Experienced merchant seamen were in demand, and we were given a choice either to ship out or to join the army.

The nation's draft boards now controlled our lives. We knew that we could be called for induction into the armed forces at a moment's notice. But shipyard workers were one those groups placed in a special category because our jobs were vital to the war effort. The government was in no hurry to draft us, but because of my sea experience, I knew my days were numbered. By mid-January, I felt that I had to make a decision. After talking to my some of my Lincoln Brigade comrades, I decided against the army. I heard that some veterans who volunteered earlier had been mistreated by the commanding officers of their units. We veterans later found out that we were officially classified by our own government as "premature anti-Fascists," a phrase that defied all logic.

At the NMU hall, I ran into some of my old shipmates who told me about a new federal training program under the U.S. Maritime Service that allowed experienced seamen to become licensed merchant marine officers. In addition to American citizenship and good health, the program required a minimum of three years deck or engine room experience on American merchant vessels. I easily met the requirements and seized this opportunity. A week later I was in an ensign's uniform at the U.S. Maritime Service Training Station in New London, Connecticut.

For the next four months, I was quartered on the campus of the Coast Guard Academy on board a small passenger ship berthed at a dock on the Connecticut River. There were two men assigned to each stateroom. My roommate was Nate Cohen, a good union man, as were most of the others on board, including a few from the 1936 Spring Strike: Frank Sciavo, Joe Ramos, Hal Berlin, and Lee Ariel, an Annapolis dropout who helped us master the fine points of celestial navigation.

We were free on weekends, and most of us took the train into New York to be with family and friends. On Sunday afternoons, the gang rode the train from Grand Central Station to New London in time to beat the curfew. For the most part we were a well-disciplined group of future mates and engineers, though there were a few who tried to drown their problems in alcohol. I graduated with honors in time for me and Sonia to celebrate our first wedding anniversary.

Now I had a Third Mate's license and was eligible to join the National Association of Masters, Mates and Pilots, an AFL union that was not especially militant. Nevertheless, I joined and registered to ship out. With

Sonia pregnant and me about to return to submarine-infested seas, we decided to move back with my in-laws in New Jersey. Before I was called to active duty, Sonia and I spent two weeks vacationing at Briehl's Farm in Walkill, New York.

Dairy farmer Fred Briehl worked seven days a week from sunup to sundown, and yet he found time to socialize and engage in political discussions every evening after milking his cows. Fred and his wife Edna ran a kind of resort in their farmhouse, with Edna doing most of the cooking. She also joined in the evening discussions. The secret behind their energy was a shared dedication to socialist ideals, much like that which bonded Sonia and me. During the 1940s, Fred had been the Communist Party candidate for New York State Comptroller and received a substantial number of votes. He remained convinced that one day the majority of the American people would be ready for socialism, and on that point we were all in agreement.

We thought socialism was the wave of the future. Fifty years ago, sitting around the big dining table at the Briehl's farm, confident in our views, none of us could have imagined the staggering complexities of the world today. Back in 1942, we were so absorbed by the struggle to defeat Fascism that there wasn't time to think about much else other than having to make a living. After two weeks with the Briehl's, Sonia and I returned home, and I began to look in earnest for a ship.

At the end of June, I received my first assignment as a licensed deck officer. The ship was the *SS Zacapa* of the United Fruit Company's "Great White Fleet." Once aboard, I headed straight for the skipper's room to introduce myself as the new Third Mate. When I knocked on the door, a deep voice with a Scandinavian accent invited me in. Working at his desk, the old man sat in a swivel chair with his back to me. When he swung around to greet me, we were both in for a surprise. He was Captain Lars Hansen, the former skipper of my first ship. Eleven years had passed since my days as a cadet on the *Surinam,* but he recognized me immediately and quipped, "Cullinen! I thought you'd never make it!"

We sailed for Halifax to become part of a North Atlantic convoy. After laying at anchor in Halifax for several days waiting for more ships to join us, we finally headed out past the Grand Banks of Newfoundland. We were bound for Liverpool. There were about thirty ships in the convoy, most of which we rarely saw because of the dense fog. It was difficult to maintain assigned positions in such poor visibility. Each vessel trailed a fog buoy on a long line from the stern. All we could see most of the time was the white plume of sea water being thrown up by the buoy. The trick was to keep the ships equidistant at all times, which required endless pinpoint adjustments in course and speed.

I didn't envy Captain Hansen. Although navigating the vessel was primarily the responsibility of the mate on watch, the old man was on the bridge much of the time. He was an impressive sight standing on the wing of the bridge, with his white walrus mustache stained yellow from snuff. As his new Third Mate, I soon gained his trust with my abilities as both sailor and navigator. Concerns for the safety of his ship were more than justified, as we were in constant danger of being torpedoed by German U-boats, a threat that haunted us throughout the voyage. There were also icebergs to be avoided in the heavy fog. Destroyer escorts from the Canadian Navy patrolled the area around the convoy and gave us some sense of security. They accompanied us about halfway across the Atlantic, and then their British counterparts took over until we arrived safely in British territorial waters.

At the end of 1942, Sonia gave birth to our daughter, Cydney. Now a father, I wanted to stay ashore. For a few months, we managed on money I earned as a night relief officer on ships docked in the port of New York. Later my cousin Basil helped me enter an aerial navigation training program with American Export Airlines. The company had a contract with the U.S. government to fly vital material to our armed forces in North Africa. They were looking for merchant marine officers who could be trained to switch from marine to aerial navigation. I was hired as a trainee and sent to navigation school in Queens.

The transition from surface to aerial navigation is actually quite simple. There is little difference in plotting the position of an airplane moving at a speed of three hundred knots and a ship averaging twelve knots. The methods of celestial navigation and dead reckoning apply to sea and air, though as flight navigators we used different instruments and terms to determine course, speed, and so on. Essentially, I switched from the sextant to a bubble octant. We took training flights over Long Island Sound in airplanes that were clumsy-looking, flying boats, PBY's (Catalinas) and PB2Y3's (Coronados). Fortunately, they flew well and there was plenty of room on board to move around. The crew consisted of pilot, co-pilot, engineer, navigator, radio operator and an instructor from the navigational school.

In the spring of 1943, we trainees had to apply for passports to fly overseas. Two weeks after I applied, I received a letter from the State Department that stated, "After careful consideration of your case, we cannot issue you a passport at this time." Though I might have expected it, I was shocked with the realization that my own government was still attempting to punish anti-Fascists as a matter of policy. My boss, D. G. Richardson, vice president in charge of operations, kindly allowed me to remain on the payroll while I appealed my case. I was given a special assignment servicing the navigation equipment on outgoing planes through the winter and spring of 1944. Then my cousin tried to assist me by arranging for me to see a special investigator named Straley, a professional witch hunter for the Texas Company. The interview was fruitless and ended after I asked him what side he was on in the war.

A short time later, Basil introduced me to one of his former subordinates who was doing intelligence work for the Air Force. I met Colonel Woody in Washington, D.C. and he volunteered to go to bat for me at the State Department. He escorted me to the office of a minor State Department official who interviewed me. I thought my interrogator would surely be impressed by the sight of a uniformed Air Force colonel at my side. After a few minutes, I was asked me to step out of the room. When the Colonel came out a short time later, he looked crestfallen. He put his arm around my shoulder and said, "I'm sorry. I can handle the Air Force and the Army, but there's not much I can do about the Navy. Naval intelligence has filed a negative report on you." This confirmed what I had long suspected. Naval intelligence had informers in the merchant marine to report on "dangerous radicals" like me. Our government was out to get those who took the lead in fighting the shipowners for better wages and working conditions, and especially those of us who had fought against Fascism in Spain.

I thanked Basil for his efforts and returned to my job at La Guardia Airport. As a last resort, I took my case to Carol King, a New York lawyer who on more than one occasion had successfully defended Harry Bridges against deportation. She agreed to take my case pro bono, but it was not destined to be resolved by the courts. I was never optimistic about winning, so I began to study and eventually passed an exam to upgrade my license from Third to Second Mate.

I was ready to ship out again. I felt like I had been avoiding the war and not doing what I was qualified to do. Richardson agreed to help me find a ship. He sent me over to the American Export Line in New Jersey to see the company shipping master, who needed a Second Mate for the *SS Sea Owl.* This was a new C-3 troop ship which was still in the shipyard in Pascagoula, Mississippi. The shipping master wanted to fly me down immediately at the company's expense. I gladly accepted his offer, though I barely had time to pack my gear and say goodbye to Sonia.

I signed on as Second Mate on July 27, 1944. We left the shipyard and took her on a shakedown cruise up the Atlantic coast to New York, then down to Newport News to load our "live cargo," which seemed like an entire army battalion. She was a beautiful ship on the outside, but below the main deck every inch of space was filled with triple-decker bunks. It was so crowded that many of the GIs took refuge on the main deck for much of the voyage. We were part of a convoy transporting a full Army division to Naples. Our trip across the Atlantic, one day ahead of a hurricane, took two weeks.

Naples was by that time a secure base of Allied military operations. It was also a den of prostitution filled with street urchins begging for cigarettes and chocolate. Cigarettes were the primary medium of exchange, while money had little value. The only escape from the depressing atmosphere was a former club called the Crespi House, which overlooked the bay and Mount Vesuvius. I sat at its sidewalk café, talking and sharing drinks with Army officers who arrived with our convoy. From what they told me, I knew something big was in the works. Later, I learned our convoy had been part of Allied preparations for the invasion of Southern France.

I crossed the Atlantic six more times, and made a trip to Eniwetok and Guam in the winter of 1945. I was fortunate to come through unscathed. But how different my fate might have been if I had been on the Murmansk run. Like many of my former shipmates, including some veterans of the Lincoln Brigade, I might not have lived to tell the tale. The war was surely the greatest tragedy of my generation, and while the military conflict would end, the struggle for social justice would continue. Rather than recognize those of us who had first served the cause of anti-Fascism, the government would continue to discriminate against us and brand us as subversives.

Chapter Five

Surviving the Witch Hunt / 1947 - 1971

After the war, I hoped to unpack my sea bag and find a way to stay ashore. But with a growing family to support, I needed a steady income. Our daughter, Cydney, was three years old, and Sonia was pregnant with our son Robbin. At the suggestion of Sonia's parents, I went to work in their factory. The girdle and brassiere business required me to operate sewing and cutting machines, and I was doing fine until one day I was asked to deliver a load of goods to a company in Manhattan's garment district where a strike was in progress. My refusal to cross the picket line displeased my in-laws and I soon gave up my position at the factory.

I had no alternative but to return to the sea and signed on as Chief Mate on the *SS George B. McFarland* under the command of Captain J. K. Moran. I had by this time upgraded my license three times to the rank of Master (oceans). We sailed from New York in February of 1947, took on a cargo of bauxite in Trinidad and then unloaded in Rio de Janeiro. Bombay was our long-term destination, and the trip would keep me at sea for six months.

Captain Moran's sense of humor was a lifesaver on that journey. He was fond of practical jokes and often kept me company on the bridge during my evening four to eight watch. Before our arrival in Rio, he warned me about a notorious waterfront prostitute who was called the Brazilian Beast. He asked me to be on the lookout for her because she was known to sneak aboard ships in port to do business with the crew. It was my duty as Chief Officer to make sure that she was not permitted to come aboard.

On our third day docked in Rio, I was awakened from an afternoon nap when I felt someone climbing into the bunk beside me. Staring at me with a silly toothless grin was a middle-aged black woman. I blurted, "Who the hell are you?" It dawned on me at that moment that my intruder must be the Brazilian Beast. Her identity was quickly confirmed when I heard the laughter of Captain Moran and the Third Mate, who were peering into my room through the open porthole. The woman joined in the laughter, boisterously acknowledging that she was an old friend of the skipper.

We sailed from Rio bound for San Nicolas, a small university town on the Rio La Plata. The tango, the milonga, and the soothing herbal scent and taste of *matte* stay with me as memories of our six weeks in Argentina. We took on a river pilot at the mouth of the Rio La Plata to guide us upstream to San Nicolas, where we loaded a cargo of *maíz* (corn). We spent two weeks to loading down to what was considered a safe draft for that port. While we were docked, I had time to get acquainted with the town and its wild and wooly gaucho culture.

I became friendly with an older sailor named Joe, one of the oilers in our crew. He was an anti-Fascist Gallego who had miraculously obtained asylum as a merchant seaman in the U.S. after escaping from Franco's murderers in 1941. After a few beers, our conversations usually turned to Spain and the International Brigades. We also talked about the political repression we saw in Latin American third world countries like Argentina, Brazil, Uruguay and Chile. Human rattlesnakes in those nations took the form of corrupt regimes against which an uphill battle for democracy and human rights would have to be fought.

One evening while docked in San Pedro, we discussed such political topics with a group of local people who Captain Moran invited aboard for cocktails. This party turned out to be a real bash as well as an exercise in goodwill diplomacy. I remember dancing with a young Argentinian woman named Sara Gutierrez. We became friends and when we met for the last time in Buenos Aires, she gave me a copy of John Steinbeck's *Vinas de Ira* (*The Grapes of Wrath*). Sara suggested the book would help me with my Spanish, but her choice of a story about the victims of the Great Depression was also an indication of where she stood politically. She was surely one of those who would one day lend her voice to the fight for democratic reforms in her country.

Early in June, we arrived in Durban, South Africa for bunkers. I went ashore to mail a letter home and found that the post office had two entrances. One side was marked "European" and the other was "Non-European." I entered the "Non-European" side and thereby caused a bitter squabble with the postal clerk who insisted that I had entered on the wrong side. I told him, "I'm not European. I'm American." After offering me a feeble rationale for his country's racist policies, he reluctantly accepted my letter. Traveling in the city, I saw a number of rickshaws, always with white occupants being pulled along by black men wearing colorful feathers and noisy, jingling leg bracelets. They were members of the Zulu tribe, and the thought struck me that revolution was inevitable everywhere human beings were forced to live under such wretched conditions.

After an eighteen-day trip across the Indian Ocean, we arrived in Bombay. A shore gang was hired to chip, scrape and paint the hull. As we discharged our cargo of *maíz* in the tropical heat and humidity, weevils from the cargo began crawling all over the ship. My sweaty body was an irresistible target for these vermin. Sleep was nearly impossible, so I improvised an air-conditioning system with wet bath towels hung in front of an electric fan.

Soon after we arrived, one of the shore gang bosses came aboard to talk with me. He was dressed like a prosperous business man, and his mission became clear when he slipped me a few hundred *rupees,* explaining that it was the custom in India to pay *bakhsheesh* to the Chief Mate and Captain. This practice reflected the corruption-riddled legacy of British imperialism, and I wondered at the time what this gang boss expected in return. To my Western eyes, the Indian caste system was a horrific example of class exploitation. As middlemen in the shipping trade, the Indian bosses were pocketing the lion's share of the profits and paying us off to keep quiet, while the Untouchables on the dock were doing all the dirty work for a pittance. I viewed their plight the same way I saw the exploitation of merchant seamen by the owners of the steamship companies.

There was nothing to be gained by refusing the money, which I tried to put to good use when I went ashore. I saw swarms of filthy, ragged, barefoot children. Many were covered with flies that were eating away at sores on their faces. Everywhere these children tugged at my clothing and repeated over and over, *"Bakhsheesh, sahib. Bakhsheesh, sahib."* They were panhandling just as I had in the worst days of the Depression. As I walked the streets of Bombay and gave away my coins, I was distressed by the realization that my act of charity was in reality no more effective than putting Band-aids on a cancer.

The kids weren't the only ones I saw begging. Crawling on the sidewalk like a crab was a pathetic human "thing" with hands and feet half-eaten away by leprosy. His eyes were empty sockets. Dancing around this unbelievable sight and shouting to the passersby for *bakhsheesh* was a tall, bearded character who apparently owned the unfortunate leper. At first I thought he was simply a professional beggar. But as I watched people drop coins into his basket, I couldn't help but wonder if this appalling spectacle was somehow an attempt to draw attention to the misery of such unfortunate creatures. Perhaps this beggar was actually a kind of prophet or holy man.

I was introduced to another side of life in Bombay when I met Mulk Raj Anand, one of India's foremost English language writers. I contacted Mulk at the suggestion of an Indian friend of mine in New York and had dinner with him and his wife in their lovely home. His wife was a dancer well known throughout her country. Politically committed as a novelist, Mulk voiced his concerns about the exploitation of the Untouchables. Before I left their home that night, he gave me a copy of one of his books, *Two Leaves and a Bud,* a novel about the plight of workers under the thumb of British masters on a tea plantation.

I had been encouraged to visit a certain jewelry store owned by a merchant named Nanubhai. From the moment I walked in, I was treated as a special customer. Nanubhai Sahib had me sit at the counter and placed before me a dazzling display of rubies, emeralds, and sapphires. I noticed that he kept a close watch on the open store entrance. At one point, he excused himself and rushed past me just in time to discourage one of the city's many roaming cows from entering. The cows had free rein of the streets and often held up traffic. One of the many disturbing contradictions of Indian society was the fact that these animals were considered sacred by the Hindus and were actually treated with higher regard than the homeless masses who were barely able to eke out an existence on the sidewalks.

The higher caste ladies in their beautiful saris and the affluent gentlemen sipping gin slings at the Taj Mahal Hotel accepted the glaring injustice of the caste system as its beneficiaries. Their system of belief was rooted in the Hindu concepts of karma and reincarnation -- if you were a good person and accepted your place in the social order, you would be rewarded in the next life. This struck me as not very different from Christian faith in "pie in the sky when you die" and brought to mind Marx's famous aphorism characterizing religion as the opiate of the people.

Another religion I encountered in that part of India was Zoroastrianism. Its followers, the Pharisees, had temples called Towers of Silence, their high walls enclosing central courtyards. One of their religious practices was placing the bodies of their dead out in the open courtyards to be eaten by vultures. When I first heard about this ritual, I was incredulous. But one day I saw several vultures perched on the walls of a Zoroastrian temple. They were actually devouring human flesh, and during the rest of my stay, I often saw these birds lined up on the walls awaiting their next meal.

On our homeward journey, we made an emergency stop for repairs in a lagoon at the northern tip of Luzon in the Philippines. While we laid at anchor, our engineers took several days to repair the ship's propeller shaft.

The weather was unbearably hot and humid, and we were not granted shore leave as there were no docks and there was no town. We were surrounded by dense tropical jungles. Like the rest of the crew, I was relieved when we finally weighed anchor and headed north into the Japanese current carrying us beyond the Aleutian Islands. In the middle of August, one month after leaving Bombay, we passed through the Straits of Juan de Fuca into Puget Sound.

Arriving in Seattle, I was anxious to be paid off and get back to my family in New York. Six months was the longest time that Sonia and I had been separated. As much as I wanted to stay ashore with my wife and children, I was forced to ship out again and again because we needed the income. For a time I tried selling Electrolux vacuum cleaners door-to-door in the Bronx, but I wasn't cut out to follow in my father's footsteps as a salesman.

At that time, Sonia was working as Assistant Director of Les Coquelicots, a school in Great Neck that belonged to her Aunt Mary. One day Sonia suggested that she and I might like to have a school of our own, and her aunt replied, "Why not? Let's look for a suitable location, and I'll help you get started." Starting from scratch to establish a school was no simple matter. There were many practical and legal requirements. Sonia began the project without much assistance from her seagoing husband, but she was determined to bring me ashore. She and Mary found a marvelous three-story stone building on a beautiful property overlooking Little Neck Bay in Bayside, Queens. Mary helped us with the finances, and we bought the place in October of 1948.

We named the school Les Clochettes. We were under the jurisdiction of the Division of Day Care of the New York City Department of Health.

Regulations required a certified teacher to be in charge of each group of children, and a certified Educational Director to plan and supervise the program. Fortunately, Sonia managed to deal with most of the red tape before I ever set foot ashore. Her efforts were nothing short of miraculous, carried out all the while she was caring for our two young children. My wife had a plan and nothing would stand in her way. July 15, 1949 marked the end of my eighteen year seagoing career. Having found a way at last for me to stay ashore, I quit my job as Second Mate on the *SS Dean H.,* a molasses tanker.

Sonia had a great deal of experience in the theater as both performer and teacher, but she was not certified in the field of Early Childhood Education. She enrolled in Bank Street College and devoted herself to studying the administration and supervision of schools for young children. With the assistance of Professor Agnes Snyder, Sonia carried out all the planning and set up Les Clochettes with a summer program that started in mid-July. The school was fully equipped and staffed, with an initial enrollment of forty-five students, a Pontiac station wagon and an Airedale dog.

One of Sonia's friends who had taught at Les Coquelicots came to work temporarily as our first Educational Director. If we were to be financially successful in the long run, however, one of us would have to become qualified to take over. Sonia was already overburdened with the administration of the school, so I was the logical candidate to fill the position if I could meet the challenge of getting a college degree. First I had to take the test for a high-school-equivalency diploma, and then a validation examination for college entrance. Soldiers returning from the war were able to complete their education through the GI Bill, but there were no such benefits for me. Even though the merchant marine casualty rate during the war was higher than that of any branch of the armed forces except the Marine Corps, nearly fifty years would pass before these seamen were recognized by Congress and officially classified as war veterans.

In 1955, I received my bachelor's degree in Early Childhood Education at New York University. I soon took on the responsibilities of Educational Director, a position that I held for the next twenty-four years until our daughter took over. Later, I was accepted as a PHD candidate at Columbia University, but withdrew after a year at Sonia's request because she needed me full-time at the school.

Inspired by one of my N.Y.U. professors, Dr. Christian Arndt, I worked with teachers and parents to create a progressive curriculum that we called "Education for a Peaceful World Community." From the beginning, we made every effort to racially integrate both the teaching staff and the children enrolled. This was not an easy task in a white, middle-class community, but over time we accomplished a great deal. I often photographed the school's day to day activities. Naturally, parents were eager to see what programs we were offering and how their children were progressing. Near the end of each school year, we presented a slideshow of that year's activities. The discussions that followed enabled parents to better understand our educational philosophy. Most were pleased to see their children being challenged with new ideas and interacting with others in the outside world.

Our educational philosophy was considered radical and drew the attention of the powers-that-be during the McCarthy years. As a Lincoln Brigade veteran, I continued to carry the stigma of being a "premature anti-Fascist." The Veterans of the Lincoln Brigade (VALB) had been placed on a list of subversive organizations by the U.S. Attorney General in 1947 and later became a target of the Subversive Activities Control Board. Legal battles on behalf of the VALB eventually went to the U.S. Supreme Court and vindicated the organization. Despite harassment, the VALB continued to agitate for a democratic government in Spain and assisted many veterans in need. When the political climate eased in the 1970s, we supported various international causes -- assisting victims of Franco's regime in Spain, providing medical support to Nicaragua and aiding a children's hospital in Cuba.

At a certain point, FBI agents visited Sonia and me at the school and tried to question us about our activities. One of the agents asked me if I knew Harry Bridges, and I said, "Are you kidding? Everyone knows Harry Bridges!" We managed to evade the FBI, but Sonia's famous brother didn't fare as well under pressure from his inquisitors. Jerry Robbins became an informer and identified eight of his colleagues as members of the Communist Party in his 1953 testimony to the House Committee on Un-American Activities (HUAC). I remember how tormented Jerry was in the days before he was scheduled to appear in Washington. Sonia and I tried unsuccessfully to convince him not to cooperate, to tell the committee to go to Hell. But he was terrified by the threat of exposure of his homosexual lifestyle and what he saw as the likely destruction of his career. The atmosphere was one of suspicion and paranoia. After Jerry caved in to HUAC and named names, Sonia and I lost some of our friends on the left and became estranged from Jerry for a number of years.

Despite the political witch-hunting and Cold War hysteria, we managed to build a school that became known around the world. Recognition and support for Les Clochettes grew during its first decade thanks to a number of innovative projects, one of which was the initiation of a worldwide exchange of children's art. By 1962, we had accumulated a collection of children's art from forty-four countries in Europe, Asia, Africa, and Latin America. The collection was catalogued by Brenda Lowen, a graduate student volunteer. With her assistance, we organized The Children's International Art Show, which was first presented at Manhattan's Carnegie International Center and cosponsored by the United Nations Association. As a Lincoln Brigade veteran, I took special pleasure in seeing the children of Spain represented in this creative exhibition celebrating the ideal of a peaceful world community.

Chapter Six

Progressive Film-making / 1971 - 2003

I had taken some courses in filmmaking during my undergraduate years at NYU and came up with the idea of doing a documentary film about the school. In May of 1971, I started filming with the help of an Oscar-winning cameraman, Ed Lynch. I chose the title, *La Primavera* (*The Spring*), because we shot the film during the spring and our subject was children who were in the springtime of their lives. By the summer, I faced the challenge of editing four thousand feet of film.

With my limited editing experience, I turned to the Yellow Pages and found the phone number for a Manhattan film company called Artscope. When I called and explained my problem, I was encouraged by a voice with a strong Indian accent. "Come to me and I will help you." The man sounded as if he had been sitting by the phone for years just waiting for my call. This was the beginning of my friendship with Amin Chaudhri from Bombay, who taught me film editing.

"La Primavera" became an effective promotional piece for the school and our world education program. The film was a hit with the parents, who were some of our most avid supporters in the community and remained involved with us long after their children had outgrown the school. Meanwhile, I continued my studies at N.Y.U. and received an MA in Cultural Anthropology and International Education. Our work with the school paid off as there was more than enough income to cover expenses. Not only did the school pay for my education, but there was enough money for college tuition for both our children. In 1967, we bought a beautifully restored, two-hundred-year old landmark house near Vermont's Mt. Snow Ski Resort. Three years later we added a condominium in the Swiss Alpine village of Klosters, a skier's paradise. Skiing became a favorite shared pastime, and we spent more than thirty years on the slopes all over Europe, as well as the Rocky Mountains.

In 1978, I presented a paper, "Education for a Small Planet," at a conference of the National Association for the Education of Young Children in New York City. I discussed our school's international children's art exchange and the global ecological crisis. I had become increasingly aware of environmental issues and the unprecedented threat to human survival after reading the farewell speech given by United Nations Secretary General U Thant on May 9, 1969. The urgency of the ecological crisis was driven home to me in 1972 when I read *The Limits to Growth: A Report for the Club of Rome's Project on the Predicament of Mankind (by Donella Meadows, et al.).* The report came out just before the 1973 oil crisis, and the author's made a strong case that the environmental impact of human depletion of natural resources would have dire consequences for the planet unless the present rate of consumption were vastly reduced. Many in the world's scientific community feared that we might pass the point of no return unless the prevailing policies of the industrialized nation were changed rapidly.

During the 1970's and 80's, I was heartened by the advent of a worldwide grassroots movement for ecological preservation. In every industrial nation, environmental organizations began educating people about these issues, bringing pressure to bear on political leaders. In June of 1982, almost one million people demonstrated at the UN demanding an end to the arms race and the outlawing of nuclear weapons. Sonia and I were in London at that time and we joined the mass protest in Trafalgar Square. Similar demonstrations took place in France, Germany, Italy, and Spain.

During these years I became more aware that the most powerful tool for affecting social and political change is the media, especially film and television. After the success of "La Primavera," I continued to pursue filmmaking in my spare time, taking workshops and working as a production assistant on various film crews. My goal was to encourage the widest possible use of film and video to spread the truth about the global ecological crisis.

My film-making efforts were encouraged through my relationships with fellow veterans who were working in the film industry. Joe Sarno invited me to work as a production assistant on several of his independent feature films. Bill Sussman, was Vice President of M.P.O., and Milt Felson was Vice President of the Directors Guild of America. Milt introduced me to Diego de la Texera, who took me along as production assistant to shoot a documentary on Culebra Island, Puerto Rico. In July of 1970, Diego, his cameraman Ken Locker, and I flew by commercial jet to San Juan. We were joined by a sound man from Sandino Films and flew by prop plane to a small airstrip on Culebra. That night we checked into the Seafarers Hotel and the four of us shared a room together.

The next day, we began shooting, first interviewing U.S. Navy personnel at an observation post on a hill overlooking the sea. Their job was to communicate with the Navy warships engaged in target practice offshore. The targets were World War II tanks at various locations in the jungles on the island. The tanks had been painted white to make then visible from a distance. These military maneuvers created enormous problems for the island's inhabitants. Naval gunfire went on seven days a week and was destroying the local fishing industry.

On our second day of shooting, a passenger ship loaded with protesters from San Juan arrived at the dock. Several hundred people came ashore waving banners, independence flags, and placards urging the U.S. Navy to leave the island. After a short meeting at the port, the protesters marched several miles from town. A large group went into the jungle to paint the tanks green, thus making the targets invisible to the ships offshore. That night the protesters sat around a huge bonfire talking, listening to speeches and singing revolutionary songs.

We followed these events, shooting thousands of feet of 16 mm color film to cover the two-day protest. The end result was a half-hour documentary entitled *El Empiezo* (*The Beginning*). Wherever the film was shown, audiences were galvanized to take action demanding the end of this outrageous naval operation. The Navy eventually gave in to the pressure by pulling up stakes and moving to Vieques Island. I was inspired by the organizational success of both the protest and the film.

In the fall of 1979, I enrolled in an intensive 16 mm production course at the Parsons School of Design in New York City. We worked seven days a week on both sides of the camera learning every aspect of filmmaking. I began to think seriously of making another film and soon outfitted myself with a Canon Scoopic 16 mm camera, a 400-foot magazine, and a shoulder brace.

My next opportunity came in the summer of 1981 during the National Nuclear Freeze Campaign, which was supported by a number of organizations including the American Friends Service Committee (AFSC). On the fourth of July, Sonia and I marched with the peace contingent of the Independence Day parade in Brattleboro, Vermont. After the parade we were invited to a luncheon meeting where we heard a local AFSC leader, David McCauley, announce plans for a "Washington to Moscow Peace Walk." This was actually to be a three-day, 35-mile journey from Washington, Vermont to Moscow, Vermont. After hearing David's plan, I raised my hand and said, "Somebody should make a documentary film of this event." David's challenged me saying, "I agree with you, George. So do it!"

With the peace walk scheduled to begin on August 6, I barely had time to prepare. The project was going to require extensive coverage in a number of locations over the three days, and I would need help. I first turned to Alan Dater, a filmmaker in Marlboro, Vermont who volunteered to come along with his camera and a sound technician. Two other Vermonters, Mike Campbell and Robin Lloyd also volunteered to join us with their cameras and sound technicians. I asked Robin Lloyd of Burlington to join me and my camera with her sound equipment. A Mexican friend of mine, Manelik de la Parra agreed to help with sound on the last day of shooting. We made the film on the proverbial shoestring out of our own pockets. None of the professionals were paid for their work. The cause attracted many volunteers who shared our commitment to the movement.

On the morning of the second day of the protest, four hundred marchers gathered on the lawn in front of the Vermont State Capitol in Montpelier to hear a number of rousing speeches. Among the speakers we caught on film were Senator Patrick Leahy, Harvard professor John Kenneth Galbraith, and Susan Rabin of the Children's Campaign for Nuclear Disarmament. That afternoon on the outskirts of Montpelier, the marchers paused for an hour to see an outdoor anti-nuclear performance by Vermont's Bread & Puppet Theater. That evening the peace walk came to a halt in a beautiful open field in the mountains near Waterbury, where we spent the night.

The next morning, we attended a meeting in a Waterbury church. David McCauley introduced Yuri Kapralov, a representative of the Soviet Embassy who spoke in support of the Nuclear Freeze. Kapralov had originally been scheduled to speak at the end of the walk in Moscow, but the State Department barred him from visiting that town. We all had a good laugh when we saw the headline in a local newspaper: "Russian Forbidden to Go to Moscow."

Once the shooting phase of the project was completed, I was left with four thousand feet of undeveloped film. We didn't have enough money to cover the cost of processing and editing the film even after a number of our friends made contributions. The first person to come to the rescue was Irwin Young, President of DuArt Film Lab in New York City. He offered to develop the first four hundred feet free of charge and the rest at a generous discount. After deciding against a couple of prospective editors, I had the good fortune to meet Mark Robbins of the United Nations film department. After viewing the footage, Mark volunteered to edit the film but suggested that we needed to shoot more to complete the story. We soon traveled to Washington, D.C. to cover a daylong White House vigil organized by the Children's Campaign for Nuclear Disarmament. At the same time, we also shot footage of an AF of L-CIO peace demonstration.

After Mark Robbins finished the editing, we had a provocative fifteen-minute documentary. For his contribution, Mark was listed in the credits as co-producer. After its release in June of 1982, *Washington to Moscow* was shown to peace groups and on college campuses around the country with the help of the American Friends Service Committee, which bought about a dozen prints.

I later entered the film in the Hiroshima International Amateur Film Festival, a venue for independent filmmakers from all over the world. Scheduled for July 1983, the festival awarded our film the UNESCO Prize, and the festival committee invited Sonia and me to Hiroshima as its guests. We were put up at the beautiful new Hiroshima Grand Hotel. I was delighted to be back in Japan after so many years. The film screenings and award ceremony were held in a small theater, and I received a warm reception as I walked on the stage to receive my certificate and a statuette so heavy that it had to be shipped home to Vermont.

While in Hiroshima, we visited the Peace Museum and Peace Park, where groups of pilgrims from many nations gather to sit and meditate. The charred and twisted steel frame of what as once an elegant building stands in the center of the site as a haunting reminder of the awesome destructive power of nuclear weapons. The theme of the Hiroshima Festival is Peace and Reverence for Life, an appropriate dedication in a city that was destroyed along with most of its civilian population by one nuclear device dropped in 1945. The insanity of manufacturing and stockpiling such weapons continued for decades, and it was obvious to me that the only people benefiting from that madness were those profiteering human rattlesnakes -- the arms manufacturers and their stockholders.

After leaving Hiroshima, Sonia and I toured Japan for several weeks. We took a day trip to the island of Miyajima at the southern end of the Inland Sea, where mysterious wild deer roamed through a park seemingly unafraid of human visitors. We also spent several days in Kyoto where I was reminded of my youthful adventures after jumping ship in 1932. From Kyoto we took a train to the coast of the Sea of Japan, then proceeded up to Unazuki to spend a few nights in a charming Japanese inn, finally traveling on to spend our final days in Tokyo.

Our connection with Japan clicked cinematically. Our visit to Hiroshima inspired us in 1985 to launch the first Vermont International Film Festival. We decided that the theme of this event should be "Three Minutes to Midnight," a slogan borrowed from the Bulletin of the Atomic Scientists that reflected one of the burning issues of the 1980s: the threat of a global nuclear holocaust. Sonia and I had returned home from Asia at the height of the Nuclear Freeze Campaign. Most of our friends in Vermont were involved with this movement, and they began asking us questions about the Hiroshima Festival. We soon decided to organize a similar annual event in our own country.

Early in 1984, we held a series of meetings and established a nonprofit, tax-exempt foundation to sponsor the festival. With the help of Bob Schiffer and Peter Vandertuin as founding officers, we conducted a fundraising campaign to underwrite the costs. We soon rented a theater in New York for preliminary screening and judging of film entries. Marlboro College president Rod Gander donated his facilities for the culminating festival event.

The first festival took place over three days and was highlighted by twenty-five films, a seminar on the nuclear arms race and a closing award ceremony. The winning filmmakers received plaques made of Vermont slate mounted on wood and bearing the festival's peace-dove logo. On the festival's second day, we held a seminar with several scholars, including Michio Kaku, a nuclear physicist from City University of New York, and David Conrad, co-director of the Center for World Education at the University of Vermont. Thanks to David's encouragement, our next festival took place in 1987 at the University of Vermont campus in Burlington. The Vermont Film Festival has remained in that city and continues with its unique mandate each fall by presenting "images and issues of global concern."

In 1993 we hosted 160 screenings of films that treated such issues as disarmament, ecology and human rights. My wife describes the process of our growth as repeatedly "reinventing the wheel," which might also refer to our tenacity in staying with the festival through its first thirteen years. The Festival's President, Barry Snyder, expressed our guiding philosophy, "We believe that life is sacred, that injustice is not to be countenanced, that it is our common duty to keep the planet and its teeming multitude of life from harm. And we believe the work of artists play an invaluable role in not only helping us understand the complexities of political, social, and environmental realities, but to challenge us to make change."

Looking back again on my life, I can see how for me such cherished ideals in many ways trace back to Spain. I took great pleasure in the fall of 2002 when the Festival included Julia Newman's documentary film, *Into The Fire: American Women in the Spanish Civil War.* I was deeply touched when I first watched a screening of that film and saw footage of my ship, the *SS Erica Reed,* delivering relief supplies to the Spanish Republic in 1939. I was also pleased when this year's Festival, with its cinematic call for peace at a time of war, happened to coincide with international protests against the planned American invasion of Iraq.

So it is that the fight for peace and social justice continues with our love and compassion for *la gente*, the majority of the world's decent, hard-working people struggling to survive. For my part, I continue to be outraged by the corrupt bastards in positions of power who have been so successful at keeping us divided and perpetuating their control over the earth's resources. And while I scoff at puny, half-hearted efforts to deal with problems like the global ecological crisis, I am sustained by a simple truth that I have seen proven again and again since my time on the Spanish battlefield: *Un pueblo unido jamás será vencido! -- A people united will never be defeated!* It is that knowledge that inspires us to organize and work together to control our common destiny. And may that good fight continue.

Here I am at about four with my mother and grandmother.

On July 5, 1920 in Tacoma, I was evidently not very happy posing for this shot.

In Red Bluff (circa 1922) with my Uncle Andrew and brother Richard.

I'm in the center with three seafaring buddies in the mid-thirties just before leaving for Spain.

Quartermaster at the wheel of the SS Jamaica in 1941

With Sonia at the Briele's farm in Walkill, New York.

Sonia, Cydney and I at Bradley Beach, New Jersey, about 1945.

The multicultural staff of Les Clochettes in 1953.

With Sonia at Schroon Lake in 1967.

Canadian and American veterans of the International Brigades at an Amnesty Conference for Spanish Prisoners in Toronto in thc 1970's. I'm in the front row, second from the right.

A visit to the Polish Committee for Solidarity with the Spanish People, Warsaw, 1976

Sonia and I in Japan in 1983 when I received an award at the Hiroshima Film Festival.

Celebrating our fiftieth wedding anniversary in 1991.

With my brother Richard (right) and Merlin Hatfield (center) in Red Bluff in 1991.

Celebrating Sonia's birthday in Sacile, Italy in 1994.

About The Author

George Cullinen was a veteran of the Spanish Civil War and long-time social activist. During his early years as a merchant seaman, Cullinen was a militant rank and file unionist who helped organize the National Maritime Union. After fighting in Spain, Cullinen spent eighteen years at sea; he later survived the McCarthy witch hunt, and went on to study at New York University, where he received his BA degree and an MA in cultural anthropology and international education. With his wife, Sonia Robbins Cullinen, he directed a progressive children's preschool. In 1983, he won a Hiroshima Award for his work as a filmmaker, and with his wife established the Vermont International Film Festival. Cullinen died on March 3rd, 2003 and is survived by his wife and two children, Cydney and Robbin.

Printed in the United States
16133LVS00005B/352-372